Please return to
Alice Ann Byrne P
227 E Mission
Spokane

GOD'S BELOVED

325-2686

GOD'S BELOVED

Jesus' Experience of the Transcendent

Bernard J. Cooke

Trinity Press International
Philadelphia

First Published 1992

Trinity Press International
3725 Chestnut Street
Philadelphia, PA 19104

Library of Congress Cataloging-in-Publication Data

Cooke, Bernard J.
    God's beloved : Jesus' experience of the transcendent /
Bernard J. Cooke.
        p.   cm.
    Includes bibliographical references and index.
    ISBN 1-56338-020-X paperback
    1. Jesus Christ—Spiritual life. I. Title.
BT303.C72   1992
232.9'04—dc20   91-38773
                                                                CIP

CONTENTS

PREFACE

For a Christian theologian, the fundamental question with which he or she must grapple is the one Jesus proposed to his immediate disciples: "Who do you say that I am?" Whatever response one gives to this question underpins and permeates his or her entire understanding of Christianity—indeed, his or her understanding of oneself, of human life, of human history, and of God. This question has assumed an urgency in today's world beyond what it has had for centuries largely because of Christianity's exposure to the rich traditions of other great world religions, and because modern science and technology have laid claim to be alternatives and more satisfactory responses to human needs and potential.

But if modern critical thought and scientific methodologies have challenged traditional understandings of Jesus, they have also provided the Christian theologian with tools to deal with and profit by the challenge. It is, then, the intention of this volume to draw upon the scholarly research that has been achieved in biblical studies, in historical and sociological studies of Christian origins, and in the psychology of religious experience in order to under-stand a bit more clearly and accurately the reality that was Jesus of Nazareth.

More specifically, this book will focus on Jesus' own experience of the divine, on his awareness of God as his "Abba." The reason? Here, if anywhere, one can discern the distinctive understanding of the divine that Christianity claims to have derived from Jesus. In many ways the undertaking is difficult, perhaps foolish, since it is obviously unclear whether it is possible for us in the late twentieth century to probe the awareness of someone who lived two millennia ago in a culture quite different from our own. Yet to admit total defeat is to concede that Jesus cannot ultimately be normative for Christianity as a way to God.

Since this book flows from more than sixty years of trying to respond to the question, "Who do you say that I am?" it is impossible to identify all those upon whom it depends and to express my indebtedness to them. My hope is that in some small measure it may reflect the wealth of understanding they have opened up for me and may serve to pass on some of that wealth to others. For the opportunity to do that I am grateful to Trinity Press in the person of its editor, Dr. Harold Rast. His interest and care in expediting the book's editing and publication has removed much of the burden of authorship.

1

JESUS' ABBA EXPERIENCE

To describe anyone's religious experience, even one's own, is at best a difficult enterprise. To describe it adequately is impossible. To describe the religious experience of Jesus of Nazareth is a particularly hazardous undertaking, one that a large segment of the world of biblical scholarship does not think is feasible. Still "the whole issue of Jesus' self-consciousness and its significance is one which has remained at the forefront of NT christological study more or less throughout the past two centuries."[1] An indication that interest in this study has not waned is the current discussion by study groups in both the American Academy of Religion and the Society for Biblical Literature, whose joint insights were published in a 1984 issue of Semeia.[2]

Besides, two thousand years of Christian faith have assumed that Jesus possessed some special understanding of the divine, that he communicated that insight by his public teaching and private instruction of his disciples (which were privileged "word of God"), and that his words and deeds bequeathed to humans a fuller and definitive revelation about God and about humans in relation to God. This traditional faith presumes some continuity with Jesus' own awareness of the divine and therefore some possibility of drawing upon Jesus' religious experience.

Rather than attempt a complete review of recent efforts to deal with Jesus' awareness of self in relation to the divine, let me selectively report on six present-day students of the matter, briefly describing their positions at this point and then engaging them, implicitly or explicitly, as conversation partners in the remainder of the chapter.[3]

1

① **Joachim Jeremias.** Probably no name is more closely associated with study of Jesus' religious experience than that of Joachim Jeremias. While his work on the eucharistic words of Jesus and on the parables inevitably dealt with Jesus' consciousness, it was in his *Abba* and *Das Vater-Unser* that he studied in detail Jesus' understanding of and attitude toward God.[4] His conclusions have drawn mixed reaction, particularly his remark that "there is not a single example of the use of *abba* (without a suffix) as an address to God in the whole of Jewish literature."[5] There is less denial of his conclusion that Jesus himself used Abba regularly as his form of addressing God in prayer, that he introduced his close disciples to his understanding of God as Abba, and that this use was distinctive of Jesus in his time. Jeremias goes further than most of the exegetes who agree in general with his study: whereas most would prefer to say that Abba was *distinctive* and characteristic of Jesus but not absolutely unique, Jeremias leans toward the usage as *unique* and accepts the implications of this position. "We have thus established the emergence of a completely new manner of speaking which at the same time reflects a new most profound relationship with God."[6]

② **Jacques Guillet.** Guillet's approach in *The Consciousness of Jesus* is very different from Jeremias's typically German "wissen-schaftlich" style, but his conclusions are very close to those of Jeremias.[7] Though an accomplished exegete, Guillet does not pursue a technical style in his book, nor does he restrict himself methodologically to critical textual evidence. He draws, with acknowledgment, from the best of critical scriptural research, but does so in a more contemplative manner.

Guillet does not go so far as to attribute to Jesus a clear understanding of *divine* sonship, but he joins Jeremias in granting Jesus a unique awareness of God as his Abba and therefore of his own privileged relationship to God. Moreover, he adds a couple of interesting insights that are distinctive to his book: (1) He contends that the early Christian attribution of "Son of God" to Jesus did not come by way of reference back to any specific word usage of Jesus himself, but rather as a conclusion distilled from the entire context of Jesus' sayings and deeds. (2) He argues convincingly that Jesus' human self-discovery developed in conjunction with his reading of the Bible.[8] Theologically, Guillet accepts the strictly divine character of Jesus' sonship; he contends that Jesus knew that he was uniquely Son of God, but that only gradually did Jesus in his human career come to realize the depth of this sonship. Guillet is not clear about the extent to which the full implication of this identity was recognized by Jesus prior to his death.

W. Marchel. Prior to Jeremias's two studies mentioned above ③ and also to Guillet's book, W. Marchel's doctoral dissertation at the Biblicum in Rome had investigated in great detail the question of Jesus' use of Abba.[9] After studying the antecedent Jewish use of the word, he acknowledged the distinctiveness in Judaism of Jesus' use of Abba to address God, and he agreed with Jeremias that Abba is the term by which Jesus constantly addressed God in his prayer. The one text exception is Mark 15:34, Jesus' words on the cross, "My God, my God ...," but here the words of Jesus are a quotation of Psalm 22.[10] Abba is also the term used by Jesus in all of the teaching where he refers to "his" Father.[11] Marchel finds Jesus' use of Abba to address God not only distinctive but unique in his Jewish context. However, it is in the exegesis of Matthew 11 that he goes beyond Jeremias, asserting that this text indicates that Jesus "in invoking God with this title (Abba) manifests his awareness of the personal and absolutely unique relation he has with God, a bond so close that it unites him with God as his own Father."[12] Marchel wishes to go even further than this, for he says of the awareness of Jesus reflected in Matthew 11 that it is the awareness that Jesus as the Son of God had always possessed.[13]

James D.G. Dunn. More cautious conclusions were drawn by the ④ English exegete James Dunn. In his 1975 study, *Jesus and the Spirit*, and later in *Christology in the Making* (1980), Dunn discussed at length the question of Jesus' sense of sonship.[14] Working from previous research, particularly that of Jeremias, Dunn concentrated on the extent to which Jesus had an awareness of being *the* Son of God. Though he judged that Jeremias went beyond the textual evidence, Dunn agreed that Jesus constantly used Abba in

*I felt such an intimacy w. God ⌉ only appropriate words
such an approval by God ⌋ "Abba" & "Son"
dependence on,
responsibility to

addressing God, and that this distinguished Jesus "in a significant degree from his contemporaries."[15] Jesus' use of the term "expressed a sense of sonship, indeed, on the basis particularly of Mark 14:36, of intimate sonship."[16] Further, Dunn contended that Jesus "sensed an *eschatological uniqueness* in his relationship with God . . . as the son who had the unique role of bringing others to share in the kingdom to which he had already been appointed."[17]

At the same time, Dunn is clear that no New Testament evidence, not even the Johannine claims for Jesus' *divine* sonship, can lead to the conclusion that Jesus himself was conscious of more than human identity. "If we are to submit our speculations to the text and build our theology only with the bricks provided by careful exegesis we cannot say with any confidence that Jesus knew himself to be divine, the pre-existent Son of God."[18]

A distinctive feature of Dunn's approach is his stress on Jesus' *experience* of sonship, one that went beyond intellectual conviction. Speaking of Jesus' awareness of being "son," Dunn states that the term "expresses an experienced relationship, an existential relationship, not a metaphysical relationship as such . . . (he) felt such an intimacy with God, such an approval by God, dependence on God, responsibility to God, that the only words adequate to express it were 'Father' and 'son'."[19]

⑤ **E. Schillebeeckx.** Equally measured in its conclusions was the study of Jesus' Abba experience in Schillebeeckx's *Jesus*. By common admission, this is the most detailed theological study of Jesus' religious experience. The merit of the study is that, though Schillebeeckx draws extensively from and is guided by studies that had worked from key texts in which Jesus speaks of Abba, he examines the entire career of Jesus to discover the way in which it is the expression of Jesus' awareness of his Father. At the end of this lengthy examination, concentrating on the synoptic traditions, Schillebeeckx concludes: "The Abba experience would appear to be the source of the peculiar nature of Jesus' message and conduct, which without this religious experience, or apart from it, lose the distinctive meaning and content actually conferred on them by Jesus."[20] Schillebeeckx stresses the fact that Jesus' teaching and public ministry were dominated by the reality of God, his Abba. Speaking of Jesus' public activity, Schillebeeckx says, "The heart and centre of it all appeared to be the God bent upon humanity . . . The living God is the focus of this life."[21] While he postponed a discussion of Jesus' unique identity for a later section of his massive book and even beyond that to the two subsequent volumes, Schillebeeckx certainly regarded Jesus' experience as distinctive. "Jesus' Abba experience is an immediate awareness of God as a power cherishing people and making them free . . . That is why trying to delete the 'special relation to God' from the life of Jesus at once destroys his message and the whole point of his way of living; it amounts to denying the historical reality of 'Jesus of Nazareth'."[22]

One of the characteristics of Schillebeeckx's treatment, something the present study hopes to expand, is his stress on Jesus' awareness of God rather than on the question of Jesus' awareness of his own divine identity. Such a shift is faithful to modern exegetical work, which has made clear that Jesus' teaching was entirely occupied with witnessing to the reality of his Abba and contained practically nothing about himself except by way of implication.

Jan Sobrino. Typical of liberation theologians, Sobrino locates his discussion of Christology and specifically of Jesus' consciousness within the context of God's liberating establishment of the kingdom.[23] Thus the emphasis is on Jesus' consciousness of mission, of being the chosen instrument for overcoming oppression. Clearly, this highlights Jesus' role as paradigm for those committed to building a world of justice, equality, and peace, that is, the beginnings in history of God's kingdom which will eventually reach its eschatological fulfillment.

For Jesus, the awareness of God focused (in Sobrino's view) on the process of the kingdom's emergence, for Jesus the Father was the God of the Kingdom. The 'other' required for all true prayer was not merely some abstract deity, nor even a 'personal' deity with whom one could dialogue. For Jesus it was a person whose reality could not be divorced from the kingdom he was fashioning."[24] Sobrino does not argue against Jesus' direct and intimate

5

Gethsemane scene: trust

awareness of his Father; indeed he argues, as do others, from Jesus' _trust_ in his Abba in the Gethsemane scene and from the pervading self-surrender of Jesus to his Abba's will.[25] Both of these witness to a unique relationship of love which was the foundation of Jesus' self-identity and his sense of mission.

Finding this measure of agreement among recognized scholars does not mean that one can dismiss lightly the problems proposed by critical scholarship, for the questions raised are serious and basic and must be addressed with honest respect for the results of careful textual and historical criticism. Religious convictions, cherished as they are, cannot substitute for the role played by proven methods of research or for logic in one's reflection. On the other hand, faith-claims cannot be verified or disproved by research or reasoning, though they must be solid enough to be exposed to and, if necessary, be corrected by serious historical or textual study. Indeed, mature Christian faith will welcome such aids to more accurate understanding of the Christ-event. At the same time, it is not a responsible exercise of critical thought to assume that faith-claims must be wrong or at least undeserving of serious intellectual consideration simply because they are faith-claims.

The hesitations of scholars would not be so pronounced—as they are not in dealing with other ancient historical figures whose "biographies" are ideologically influenced—were it not for the fact that Christian claims about this Jesus reach to the statement that he is the divine Son of God. Which leads us to the crucial questions, many of them badly formulated over the centuries, about Jesus' religious experience. (1) Did he have simultaneously human and divine knowledge of the godhead? (2) Did he grow in his human understanding of God? Did he know that he himself was the divine Son of God? (3)

Clearly, there is no possible starting point for careful response to such questions other than the reality of Jesus' own historical experience. And within that experience, which manifestly was that of a Jewish male experiencing life and Jewish religious faith in the context of ancient Galilee, the key element of distinctiveness had to do with what is referred to as Jesus' "Abba experience," that is,

6

JESUS' ABBA EXPERIENCE

his awareness of God as specially known and related to him in familiar immediacy. Even though the topics we will pursue in later chapters—Jesus as prophet, as male, as Jewish, etc.—are (relatively) less controversial and might help prepare for discussion of Jesus' Abba experience, they are facets of an experience that was rooted in Jesus' awareness of God and controlled by it. To study them apart from this central element of consciousness would be to render them abstract and therefore distorted. So it is with this topic that we begin our search, hoping to know better the "real Jesus."

Before going further, it might be good to deal in a preliminary way with two fundamental issues that bring into question this book's central thesis: (1) Did Jesus actually refer to God as Abba? (2) Did the application of Abba ("my Father") carry with it in Jesus' culture the overtones of an intimate loving relationship?

In response to the first question, I think the evidence points very strongly to Jesus' use of the term "Abba," but even more strongly to the kind of experience that has been associated with it. The very cautious statement of John Meier in *The New Jerome Biblical Commentary* seems hard to dispute.[26] After reviewing arguments pro and con, he concludes that "the tradition history of *Abba* probably runs from the historical Jesus to the Christian use echoed in Paul, rather than vice versa. Otherwise, we would have to invent another origin for the early Christian use of *Abba*, after ignoring the obvious one . . . On the whole, though, one is justified in claiming that Jesus' striking use of *Abba* did express his intimate experience of God as his own father and that this usage did make a lasting impression on his disciples."

The second question is more challenging. Anthropological study of Jewish family life in Jesus' day suggests that the father stood somewhat outside the structures of personal intimacy and loving support. These more affectionate relationships generally dealt with mother/children intimacy or with care and communication among brothers and sisters. The father usually "remains an authority figure mainly concerned with his family's honor and proper maintenance."[27] Consequently, even the more familial term "Abba" would not by itself argue to the love relationship that

GOD'S BELOVED

existed between Jesus and God. Instead, that relationship is reflected in the whole of Jesus' teaching and healing. To some extent, Jesus' experience of God as "lover" stood in his culture in tension with the notion of God as "father," rather than being derived from it.[28]

I wish to include a word about my approach, use of terms, and presuppositions.

This book is written within the context of the faith in Jesus of Nazareth that has been shared by the Christian community for roughly two millennia; a faith that has been quite disparate over the centuries, as the disputes about Christology make clear; a faith that has been challenged anew today because of the rise of the scientific mentality and the exposure of Christians to the other great world religions. At the same time, it will attempt (1) by the use of careful textual and historical study to discern as accurately as possible the underlying awareness of God that permeated the actual experiences that made up Jesus' career, and (2) to unpack the implications of this awareness. Obviously, this will involve first and foremost a study of New Testament texts with all the well-known difficulties of using faith documents produced by second- and third-generation Christian communities to discover the factuality of Jesus of Nazareth.

Clearly, the New Testament writings, especially the Gospels, draw from the early Christians' *memory* of Jesus, a memory that has been colored and fleshed out by the profoundly revisionist experience of the resurrection and by the communities' experience of Christ's abiding presence in his Spirit. Despite this "addition," the core memory of "the real Jesus" was carefully preserved for at least two reasons: (1) the Christians' devotion to this Jesus who was and still remained their beloved friend, and (2) their belief that Jesus as he actually was functioned as an ultimate word spoken to them by God. At least part of the motivation that lay behind the production of the four Gospels was the desire to safeguard the authentic memory of the Jesus who lived and worked in their midst and who then died and rose. So despite the attention that must be given to specific texts in the Gospels, my basic argument will not be grounded in details or particular words except insofar as these

point to the underlying Christian memory of a human who was ✱
uniquely close to God and whose use of the term "Abba" to express
this closeness (allowed them daringly to use this same term in their *We dare to say...*
prayer.

2. The term "religious experience" can have different resonances
for different people, so let me state the way it will be used in this
study of Jesus. Most importantly, the term points to the awareness
that one has of the transcendent reality that is commonly referred
to as "God." But inseparable from this is the awareness that one *also awareness of one's world*
has of oneself and of one's "world" in relationship to this transcen-
dent. Because it is so central to one's overall consciousness, this
awareness has emotional, imaginative, affective, and intuitive as
well as structured cognitive dimensions; and while one can distinguish these elements, it is impossible to disentangle them—as it is
in the case of knowing a very dear friend. So in studying the
religious experience of Jesus, we will need to examine his deepest
levels of self-understanding, the understanding of God he expresses by the use of Abba, and the context of experience in which both
of these understandings emerged. At the same time, I intend to
concentrate on *the awareness that Jesus had of God*, the awareness that
led him to address God as his Abba, to teach about God in the way
he did, and to carry on his ministry in the way he did.

3. Since I will reflect theologically on the implications of the
historical and textual "data," I will inevitably work from certain
theological and/or philosophical presuppositions. It may well be
that, despite efforts to bracket them, some will creep into my
historical and textual work, as I believe some such presupposition
enters into any exegete's or historian's "objective" research. Let me
therefore state at the beginning some views that I believe are critical
to the present inquiry. *Language: "person" "word"*

(a) Using "person" of the transcendent is, I believe, much too
uncritically accepted. It seems to me that there are only two possible valid grounds for using this word and idea about the divine:
either by way of *strict analogy*, implying that one gives to personhood a status as one of the transcendental characteristics of being
itself (which I see as dubious); or working from the *belief* that Jesus

Jesus is a word of the divine

truly functioned in his personal being, in everything he humanly was, as a word of the divine. The present study will pursue the second approach.

(b) I would wish to preserve for the notion of "word," especially when it is used in a context with trinitarian overtones, a strictly *functional* implication. However, this need not imply opposition to an *ontological* meaning for the term when applied to God, for I consider the distinction (between functional and ontological) non-operative and misleading when dealing with the transcendent. Philosophical reflection indicates that it is a distinctive aspect of the transcendent that *agere* and *esse* coincide.

Jewish understanding not fit—

(c) In the context of Christian theology, I think that the distinction between God-in-self and God-in-relation can be misleading, since at the heart of trinitarian reflection is the insight grounded in revelation that being at its absolute, that is, God, is essentially relational. This means that there is something about the divine, something that is not merely a projection of our thinking, that corresponds to our notions of God as creating, revealing, loving, etc. So Christians believe that the divine Logos, though not totally identical with God, is eternal and strictly divine.

Being relational = inter-Being

(d) When theologizing about such matters, we must beware of carrying our understandings of "distinction" to God; we are strictly unknowing about the manner in which "distinction" can occur in the utter simplicity of transcendence. The Word *incarnated* as Jesus is clearly distinct from Abba; and the Word which Jesus incarnates—not simply expresses or contains—is a real "aspect" of God.[29] At the divine level there must be something like coincidence *and* distinction between what become distinct in creation, that is, in the man Jesus. It is he who by being this distinctive human, Jesus of Nazareth, reveals the richness of divine reality.

note: 1. 2.

Abba as Lover and Beloved

love relationship

Throughout the Gospels runs the constant presumption of God's loving choice of Jesus, and all Jesus' teaching and actions reflect the awareness of his Abba's special love for him. It is this love relationship

love relationship animates his behavior

JESUS' ABBA EXPERIENCE

that animates his activity; it is this awareness of his Father as loving
that infuses all his teaching about "the kingdom of God"; and it is
fidelity to this love that leads him to the final witness of Calvary.
Jesus' experience of the divine is primarily of a creative lover,
whose Spirit/power works to save and free and fulfill and enrich,
whose compassion is grounded in empathetic understanding of
the human condition. But his experience includes also the awareness that this love is directed to himself in a <u>distinctive</u> way; he is
the beloved, the *agapetos* addressed in the baptism scene; so Abba
is not just a Father; Abba is *his* Father.

Jesus sees himself as the Beloved. distinct!

However, Jesus' awareness of God is more than that of being
specially loved; it is the experience of his Abba's supreme loveableness. In any mature love relationship, while one finds it profoundly
satisfying and exciting and assuring to be the object of another's
love, the focus of one's awareness is not one's own being loved but
the person one loves. It is a mistake to fall in love with love itself;
in genuine mature love one falls in love <u>with another person.</u> So
through the texts of the New Testament, even though once or twice
removed from Jesus' own words and deeds, there shines Jesus'
loving absorption—one might be tempted to say "obsession"—
with his Abba.

Sees Abba as supreme loveableness ✓

That this is <u>basic to Jesus' self-identification</u> seems hard to
dispute. While other elements of that self-identity, such as being
the eschatological prophet or being the Son of Man, may have
become more cognitively formulated in Jesus' consciousness—that
we will have to study later—the <u>experience of loving and being
loved by his Abba</u> seems to have <u>transfused</u> the entirety of Jesus'
life experience.

loving + being loved

Two <u>scenes</u> in the Gospel narrative might be examined as witness to this exposure of Jesus in intimate immediacy to the reality
of God: the baptism at the Jordan and the prayer of Jesus in
Gethsemane—the first describing God's "address" to Jesus as
agapetos and the second witnessing to Jesus' anguished turning to
his Abba at the prospect of impending death. The two scenes are
textually connected, a connection that becomes evident in reference to a third scene, the transfiguration, that itself witnesses to the

*3 Gospel Scenes — Baptism words
Gethsemane 3 friends
Transfiguration words, 3 friends*

11

reality we are attempting to probe. The "words from heaven" obviously connect baptism and transfiguration; the presence of the three closest disciples connects transfiguration and Gethsemane.[30]

Baptism

Jesus Baptized at the Jordan

In approaching the Gospels' account of Jesus' baptism, one is immediately confronted with the complex interpretation placed on the event by early Christian traditions and by the Gospel authors. As we will have occasion to see later, the accounts of the baptism are among the most highly theologized passages in the New Testament. This would seem to place a special burden on one who wished to use them to argue to Jesus' awareness of God, of himself, and of his mission as he was being baptized by John. However, there are certain "bare-bones" elements underlying the narrative that most probably carry us back to the actual occurrence; these converge in Jesus' sense of being uniquely loved by the God he experienced as his Abba.

Mark   Particularly in the Markan version, and most likely in the earlier traditions from which it draws,[31] the theophany that follows the actual baptizing ("as Jesus came out of the water") points to the immediacy of Jesus' awareness of God. Though "the heavens were opened" may have literary connections with apocalyptic literature of the day,[32] its import in the Gospel text is to suggest that the barrier of the firmament that separated the divine and created realms was removed, so that direct communication could occur. Jesus "hears" God's own self-communication; he is aware of the presence of God's own Spirit.

Clearly, Jesus' experience—the experience also of others, if one takes as more historically accurate the accounts of Matthew and Luke where the voice and Spirit phenomena were observed by others as well as by Jesus—is that of *someone*. It is not just that there were words spoken; someone, presumably God, spoke the words. Moreover, the notion of Spirit being sent from God would have been meaningless to Jews of Jesus' day except in terms of a *personal* God. The experience was one of communication taking place,

Did Moses & other OT also have this experience?

which means that God was experienced as a communicating self, a person. We are dealing here not with any reflection on Jesus' part, nor for that matter on the New Testament writers' part, about the ontological aspects of divine personhood. Simply, Jesus is being addressed by that divine person whom he knew intimately as his Abba. *already?*

According to all of the Gospel accounts, Jesus experienced God as revealing his special love for him: "You are" (or in the Matthean version, "this is") "my dearly beloved one in whom I delight." It is true that the Greek *agapetos* carries us back, by editorial intent, to Isa. 42:1, and so typologically identifies Jesus as the Servant of Yahweh. It is also true that it stands in apposition to *huios*, and so carries not only the more precise meaning of "beloved son" but perhaps also implications of "only begotten son."[33] And if Feuillet's connection of the baptismal scene with Isa. 44:2 and 62-64, which speak of Israel as Yahweh's son, is justified, Jesus is being described typologically as the embodiment of Israel.[34] But *Jesus is Israel* none of this takes away from the element of a deep, loving relationship; "son" only places that love in what in Jesus' culture may have been regarded, at least ideally, as the context of most profound and engaging love. For one thing, God being revealed as "Father" clearly highlights the element of "creative giving of self," which is then reinforced in the theophany of the Spirit. What Jesus was aware of was that God was *for* him unrestrictedly and intimately. God was his Abba.

For Jesus, then, God was both lover and beloved; and like any human in a deep love relationship, Jesus would have wished to please his beloved and to know that his beloved was pleased. It is *love relationship* assurance of this which the words of the Father convey; "in you my heart takes delight." Jesus is Abba's special son by mutual choice, his and Abba's. This is a covenant that absorbs and trans- *choice covenant* forms the Deuteronomic statement of covenant demand, "You shall love the Lord your God with your whole heart and your *"You shall love w/ whole"* whole mind and with all your strength." Is this perhaps the reason why the Gospels always describe Jesus as quoting the law in its Deuteronomic form?

Isaiah

13

Finally, there is "the dove." Clearly, the mention of "dove" has to do with a manifestation of God's Spirit resting on Jesus; but beyond that simple point, there is no agreed-upon scholarly interpretation of this phenomenon.[35] One cannot simply dismiss mention of the dove as a literary device used by Mark and then by later evangelists, for "the story, including the reference to the dove, belongs to the old Palestinian Jewish Aramaic Christian tradition."[36] What may be the most acceptable interpretation is that of Leander Keck:[37] If one understands the phrase "like a dove" to refer not adjectivally to God's Spirit but adverbially to the verb "descended," it is the mode of coming upon Jesus which is like that of a dove landing. Keck argues philologically that such was the intent and construction of the earliest version of Mark, but that by the time of the Lukan version the dove is the form in which the Spirit is manifested.[38] It is this theophanic dove that has attached itself to Christian imagination about the Spirit from that time onward.

Without question, the scene of Jesus' baptism (or of the baptism and temptation, if one sees them as a unit) is one of the most thoroughly theologized passages in the New Testament literature. That this should have been is logical, for it was used from early on in that instruction for Christian baptism and may even have had some liturgical use in the early decades of the church.[39] In one version or another, Jesus is interpreted in this Gospel-initiating event in relation to Adam, Isaac, the Isaian Servant of Yahweh, the Messiah, and the people of Israel. Given this fact, it may seem that there is no possibility of arguing from a term like *agapetos* which is connected with Isa. 42:1 and which some exegetes see as a Markan or pre-Markan substitution for a more primitive version's use of *eklektos* in the context of comparing Jesus to the Servant.[40] However, just the opposite can be adduced: Mark is clearly interested in relating Jesus to the Servant, and it would have been more consistent for him to have used *eklektos* (which is the LXX word used in 42:1); instead he uses *agapetos*, which agrees more with a view that the heavenly voice is confirming Jesus' own relationship to Abba.[41] In any event, all three synoptic accounts, despite some

14

independence from one another, describe the heavenly voice calling Jesus "my dearly beloved in whom I take delight." Behind the actual texts and behind the earlier traditions which scholars try to reconstruct lay the basic understanding that in Jesus' baptism God dealt with him in a distinctly loving manner. This was reflected in Jesus' constant use of the term "Abba."

Jesus in Gethsemane   *Gethsemane*

Although textually linked with the baptism at the Jordan, the scene of Jesus in the garden is much different in tone and style. As we have just seen, the baptism passage was already highly theologized in the traditions underlying the synoptic texts, and each of the evangelists added his own distinctive theological accents. By way of contrast, one comes to Mark 14:36 with a sense that one is exposed to a raw human happening whose meaning is so enigmatic that the author of the Gospel has been content to report the tradition he inherited.

all 3 Gospels:

One of the striking features of the passage is that all three synoptic traditions describe Jesus addressing God as "Father," one of the three places in the Gospels where this occurs. It is not surprising, then, that Mark 14:36 has received special attention from those exegetes, Jeremias and Marchel in particular, who have studied Jesus' use of Abba.[42]

Father

Actually, a rather complicated process of editing by Mark, and even more so by Matthew and Luke, has produced the text as we have it. Many exegetes have been influenced by the theory of two sources, proposed by Kuhn in 1952, though few have adopted it without modification.[43] Accepting critically Kuhn's discernment of two sources, David Stanley has fleshed this out in his study of the pre-Markan interpretation of Jesus' experience in Gethsemane.[44] What he proposes as the older form of the tradition, "one of the most ancient, and consequently most precious, traditions we possess regarding the prayer of Jesus in Gethsemane,"[45] does not contain any direct words of Jesus addressed to his Father, but simply states if it were possible he might be freed from "his hour."

The second source, though it emphasizes Jesus' directives to his disciples, reports Jesus' words of prayer, "Abba, dear Father, take this cup from me. Yet not what I will but what you."

Whatever its origins, the Markan passage depicts Jesus in extreme human anguish, expressing to his Abba the emotional turmoil he is experiencing. Not unlike some of the outbursts of the prophet Jeremiah in prayer, Jesus pleads for what—as the passage itself makes clear—he knows to be impossible and, at a deeper personal level, does not wish. Without going into the disputes about the conditional agreement or disagreement of Jesus' will with that of his Father, what we can gather from the scene is the intimacy of Jesus' relationship to his Abba. Faced with all the negativities and threatening uncertainties of the moment—the prospect of suffering unto death, the apparent collapse of his ministry, the abandonment of human support—he turns to the one who, if anyone, will understand and aid. The one last faithful friend is his Abba, the supreme lover of his life, whose love for him had been an unquestioned source of his own identity. At the beginning of Jesus' passion, Gethsemane is, with the cross, the supreme witness to Jesus' trust in his Abba.[46] The synoptic texts contain no words of divine reply to his prayer, though both Mark and Matthew describe Jesus as strengthened to face his ordeal and Luke inserts the mythic remark about an angel coming to comfort him.

All that the Father has . . . If exegetes have paid special attention to Mark 14:36 because of the way in which it throws light on Jesus' prayer, they have also focused on Matthew 11 (parallel Luke 10:21) as a unique synoptic witness to the manner in which Jesus addressed this Father. An indication of the importance and distinctiveness of the passage is the decades-long dispute as to whether it was part of the original text of Matthew and whether it could, in any sense, be accepted as a saying of Jesus himself. Obviously, this had to do with the "divine" implications of Jesus' words, "All that the Father has he has given to the Son; and no one knows the Son except the Father, and no one knows the Father except the Son" (Matt. 11:27).[47]

16

obedience : an attitude of loving with complete freedom ☆

In the past two decades, however, there has been mounting recognition that the text is not simply a Matthean, much less a later, interpolative bit of theologizing.[48] For one thing, its similar form in Matthew and Luke points to its derivation from Q, which means ⑤ *source* that it belongs to an early tradition.[49] If it cannot lay claim to status as *ipsissima verba*, it at least reflects a primitive Christian recollection of Jesus' public invocation of his Father.

Without probing the extent to which Matthew 11 points to Jesus as possessing some kind of equality with his Father (for that is not exactly our purpose at this point), we can look at the way in which the scene does situate Jesus in a distinctive relationship of familiarity with his Abba. If Grundmann is correct in highlighting the affective dimension of "knowing"[50]—God's knowing humans and humans knowing God—in the religious context of Judaism at the time of Jesus, the passage deals with the same distinctive love relationship we studied in the baptismal and Gethsemane passages.

In this context, what underlies the text and its originating tradition was Jesus' own expression of his experience of his Abba *sharing self in loving communication*. As the text indicates, this sharing of self was boundless on both sides, which does not rule out the human limitations involved in Jesus' formulated cognition of the situation. Clearly, Jesus' own awareness of utter obedience to his Abba was a substantive element of the experience, but the very fact that the term "obedience" could be used for what was an attitude of loving with complete freedom points to the human love being *response* to the love Jesus experienced as coming from his Abba. *obedience*

As the text describes it, Jesus' experience of his Abba was of someone who *revealed* not just to him but to the "little ones," to those who were not confined to their own presumptions of being wise but were open to acknowledging limitation and personal dependence, and so to discovering transcendent wisdom. However, the text also indicates that Jesus was aware that his was a more immediate revelation of God as Abba and that it was he who could and was meant to introduce others to his Father. *Jesus' Mission*

He was meant to introduce others to Abba

17

Jesus' Parables—Teaching the God He Knew

If the rare texts that describe Jesus' prayer to his Abba point to his unique awareness of God, so in a somewhat less direct but not less important way do his parables.[51] One of the advantages of working from Jesus' parables is the general acceptance by scholars of their origin in the actual teaching of Jesus, with the corollary that they provide a reliable reflection of the inner awareness of Jesus. Since all Jesus' parables are intended to convey an understanding of his Abba, they are obviously a unique resource in studying his religious experience.[52]

Increasing attention has been paid to the metaphorical dimension of Jesus' parables. Ricoeur's description probably summarizes as well as any the now prevalent view: parables are a combination of metaphoric process with narrative form.[53] As a narrative metaphor, the parable points to some presumably unknown referent about which knowledge cannot be gained through ordinary denotative language. In the case of Jesus' parables, there is a two-stage process; for the parable refers immediately to "kingdom of God," which itself is a tensive symbol whose referent is "the God who acts," that is, Jesus' Abba.[54]

What this says about Jesus' awareness as he taught in parables is that the transcendent reality he knows as Abba is the same God he knows from his Jewish heritage as the one "who acts in history." We will have to say much more in a later chapter regarding this Jewish matrix of his religious experience. For now, it is enough to point out that Jesus, in attempting to communicate to his auditors his view of God, had to take account of their already existent religious understandings—the images and categories that were familiar to them, their religious experience, and their inherited traditions. So his parables were at once familiar and strange, challenging and puzzling, and therefore capable of leading to conversion. The conversion in question, though it obviously had important behavioral implications, was essentially a cognitive shift in the understanding of God. The parables drew attention to those characteristics of his Abba that were particularly prominent in *parables draw listener into his (ex) experience of Abba*

Jesus' perception of his Father and which, therefore, he wished to convey to others.

As Crossan has pointed out,[55] parables are grounded in experience; as metaphors they are meant to draw the auditor into the speaker's experience, to allow him or her to share vicariously in the experience. The parables of Jesus therefore do much more than communicate his structured cognition of the transcendent; they lead one into their originating experience, that is, into Jesus' experience of his Abba which he tries to share through narrative metaphor.[56] A sampling of parables may illuminate some aspects of his experience.

Parable of the Wicked Tenants

In many ways the most distinctive of Jesus' parables, the story of the wicked tenants of the vineyard, provides a special insight into Jesus' understanding of his prophetic mission, and we will have to study that aspect of it in a later context.[57] It is also one of the passages where there seems to be a special application of "son" (*huios*) to Jesus, with possible implications of divine sonship, with the result that its authenticity has been frequently contested— though present-day scholarship is almost universal in attributing at least the main portion of the parable to Jesus himself and in viewing it as an allegorical portrayal of the history of Israelitic prophetism.[58]

For the moment, however, our interest in the parable is the manner in which it portrays the God of Israel, Jesus' Abba. While the parable ends with the "owner's" condemnation of the Jewish leadership, the underlying picture of God emphasizes the patience with which God has dealt with humans' refusal to cooperate with him and the willingness of God to "go the extra mile," even to the point of sending his own Son in the hope of finally converting the tenants of the vineyard.

Though a few scholars contest the link with Isaiah 5, it is very difficult to see how a Jewish auditor of the parable could not have recalled immediately that passage with its poignant "song of the vineyard." It is true that "vine" as a metaphor for Israel is used in many Old Testament passages, but the detailed paralleling of Mark 12:1-12 (Matt. 21:33-46, Luke 20:9-19) to Isaiah 5 is too striking to have avoided notice. At one point, however, the progression of the "argument" as found in Isaiah shifts in Jesus' parable: When God asks the question, "What more can I do for my vineyard?" the Isaian response is, "Nothing, therefore the vineyard (Jerusalem) is to be left desolate." But the unexpected statement in Mark 12:6 is, "I will send my own son, surely they will respect him."

It is this changed viewpoint about the divine reaction to human sinfulness that reflects Jesus' awareness of his Abba. The God that Jesus knows does not wait to be appeased. This God takes the initiative to "seek and find that which was lost"; this God's attempts to win over recalcitrant humans knows no bounds; this God is one who "goes the extra mile"; only the deliberate rejection of the divine overtures by the human refusal to convert stands in the way of God's forgiveness. The parable is reminiscent of John 3:16 where Jesus says of his Abba that "God so loved the world that he sent his only Son, so that through him humans could have life."

An element of the parable that requires special attention in our present study is the use of *agapetos*: the owner of the vineyard says that he will send his own *beloved* son. This obviously recalls the use of *agapetos* in the baptismal scene and would be particularly confirmatory of Jesus' awareness of his Abba's love if the term could be traced back to Jesus himself. However, the Matthean version does not contain the word, and since even a "friendly" commentator like Snodgrass argues for the priority of the Matthean source,[59] one cannot without question use the word as an indication of Jesus' awareness of his Abba. At the very least, the application of *agapetos* to the Son in this distinctively historical parable points to the primitive communities' conviction that Jesus was God's "beloved."

Parable of the Father of the Prodigal

One of the most detailed parables of Jesus portraying the fatherly "attitude" of his Abba is that of the father of the prodigal son.[60]

20

Situated by Luke in chapter 15, which deals with "what was lost and then found" and "the joy in heaven" upon regaining what was lost, the parable is unmistakably intended to convey an understanding of Jesus' Abba as a God who stands ever ready to forgive, even taking the initiative to seek out "that which was lost." Linnemann seems to contest this by insisting that the point of the parable was to answer the Pharisees' charges about Jesus eating with sinners.[61] Certainly, the Lukan narrative does structure chapter 15 as a response to the Pharisees; but this does not militate against the parable being intended as teaching about the God Jesus experienced. Both the Pharisees' criticisms and Jesus' response deal with the nature of "the kingdom," which remains the basic metaphor throughout. Jesus' claim is that his association with "sinners" gives expression to his Abba's Spirit, which is the moving force in his own life.

The attribution of unquestioning compassion to God in the parables of Luke 15 is not weakened by the parable of the wicked husbandmen, which follows immediately in the Gospel and which ends with the vineyard owner's judgment upon the murderous tenants. As is clear from the Gospels' use of shepherd imagery, the text of Ezekiel 34 remains a strong element in the background of the early Christian image of God; and it is this text which describes Yahweh as moved with compassion for the poor and oppressed and therefore angrily condemnatory of "the big sheep" who are the oppressors.[62]

The Good Shepherd *Ezekiel 34*

It seems that it is against the background of Ezekiel 34 that the synoptic parables of shepherd and sheepfold are cast, though not in the extended form that one finds in the Gospel of John.[63] Whereas in John the parable is explicitly and immediately applied to Jesus himself, in the synoptic text (Matt. 18:12-14; Luke 15:4-7) the metaphoric reference is directly to "your heavenly Father" and only implicitly to Jesus' own activity. The purpose of the words of Jesus as contained in the synoptic text is to portray God as

*Jesus Spirit + Abba's Spirit : One. Abba's Spirit is the impetus, the creative power in Jesus + Kingdom is established Here in Jesus

GOD'S BELOVED

concerned for the least of the "little ones"—or as the Lukan version has it, "for one sinner who repents."

The Pattern of Jesus' Own Ministerial Activity

A later chapter will study in detail the healing activity of Jesus as a mirror of his experience of God as Abba and of himself in relation to his Abba. For now, a quick reflection on the way in which the understanding of God as Abba underlay Jesus' entire public ministry will round out our treatment of Jesus' experience of the transcendent as his Abba.[64] Any number of passages in the Gospels speak of Jesus' awareness that his attitudes and motivations, and the actions that flowed from them, were completely congruent with the will of his Father. What moved him as his own spirit was his Abba's Spirit, a personally creative power that was the basic eschatological impetus toward establishment of the kingdom. For Jesus there were not two parallel or linked actions, that is, God's and his; there was only the one action of Abba establishing his kingdom in and through Jesus. That was why he was so insistent that "the kingdom of God is here in your midst," that it was not simply the object of eschatological expectation.[65] That it also why it is impossible to separate Jesus' awareness of his Father's compassion, a compassion that was not "soft" but that was directed to healing persons through the creative power of love.

Only! Spirit

not "soft" compassion; creative power of love

Theological Reflection

What extension of these textual insights can justifiably be made through theological reasoning?

(1) Jesus' awareness of his Abba as faithfully loving and supremely lovable, an awareness that dominated his prayer and his teaching, was the most basic *word* communicated to him about the transcendent. As with any human, his own experience spoke more fundamentally about God than could any formulated religious explanation.

WORD ⎧ self revealing
      ⎩ spoken in Jesus' awareness of God.

What was distinctive about Jesus' experience was its intimacy ②
and immediacy. All the textual evidence points to the fact that
Jesus' knowledge of his Abba was immediate personal acquaintance. Unquestionably it was modified, limited, and interpreted by
a number of psychological influences—as is the case with each of
us in knowing a friend. Yet it was the kind of "knowing someone"
that the French language, for example, would designate by *con-
naitre* to distinguish it from *savior*, that is, "knowing about
someone."

Inevitably, this immediate awareness of God as his Abba interacted with all of the other elements that entered into his experience.
Above all, it must have interacted with the interpretations of "God" from
that came through his Jewish religious formation—through teach-   daily
ing, through formulated prayers recited at home and in the   life
synagogue, through rituals of various kinds, through the patterns
and atmosphere of life that flowed from observance of the law.
Jesus' awareness of his Abba reinforced some elements of this selective
interpretation while radically challenging others, for there were
fundamental incongruities between the Abba he experienced and ✱ ③
the God known and explained by those around him. For this
reason, theological attempts to deal with Jesus' religious experience must necessarily take into account the religio-cultural
influences that relativized even such an immediate awareness of
transcendence. This I hope to do in following chapters.

Jesus' awareness of the divine was the embodiment of the divine communi-
self-revelation; it was the embodiment of God's ⟨word⟩ about the ④ cation
divine selfhood. For that reason, the experience of God that Jesus
had was and is the very heart of the mystery of incarnation.
Keeping "word" in a functional context, that is, the function of
divine self-revealing, this word was being spoken in unique
fashion in Jesus' awareness of his Abba. All that his Father was as
"self" was unreservedly communicated in a love relationship, and
it was this love of which Jesus was aware and to which he
responded by calling the transcendent "Abba."

② The intimate awareness of God as his Abba, despite its im- ﾉ
mediacy, occurred in the context of Jesus' developing experience

23

of himself, of his relationships to others, and of his conversations with those he encountered. For this reason there was a basic limitation to the experience, for it was a human experience. At the same time it was a constantly changing and developing experience that drew from and was shaped by the memory of past experience.

Though the synoptic texts strongly suggest that Jesus himself did not go about claiming to be the unique Son of God, his constant references to his Abba confirm that he was aware of himself as the object of this special Fatherhood. The rare passage, Matthew 11, moves from this overall implicit statement of sonship to a more explicit statement. Moreover, as one reflects on the personal immediacy of Jesus' loving acquaintance with his Abba, Guillet's conclusion seems unavoidable, namely, that the awareness of God as Abba was not something Jesus acquired, but was instead the most fundamental element of awareness that shaped his self-identification from the beginnings of his human consciousness.

3. At the heart, then, of Jesus' self-understanding was the undeniable sense of being God's beloved one. No doubt this sense deepened as Jesus grew into full mature life, and took shape, as we have suggested, through the sequence of human experiences that made up his historical career. The love relationship between him and his Abba was, however, the dominant and ever-present reality that gave purpose to his human existing and actions. His mission was not an objectified task to be accomplished; it was an evolving process of carrying out what he perceived to be the will of his Father, to do always what would "please" his Father.

4. That leaves, however, a basic question that will have to be addressed in subsequent chapters on Jesus' religio-cultural situation as Jewish and male. Granted that Jesus' experience of God was that of being the unique object of divine love, why did the supreme lovableness of that God find expression as Abba? Or to put the question a bit differently, does the fact that Jesus' grounding experience of the divine apparently casts God in male and Jewish form render that experience inappropriate as a *universal* word of revelation?

2

THE GALILEAN RELIGIOUS CONTEXT

Once the premise is accepted that Jesus of Nazareth was thoroughly human and therefore culturally limited by his historical
surroundings, it becomes imperative for Christian theology to
reconstruct as far as possible the Palestinian context in which his
religious experience occurred. Even if his awareness of God was
uniquely immediate and intimate, it was unavoidably interpreted
by the images and categories that came to him with his language,
his education, and the details of his everyday first-century Galilean
Jewish experience.[1]

To describe as accurately as possible the interaction of Jesus'
awareness of the divine and the Jewish religious culture that
conditioned his human experiences, this chapter will distinguish
faith from beliefs and each of these from religious institutions. It
will understand *faith* as referring to the basic human attitude of
open and honest response to reality, however that reality is perceived; this implies an acceptance, either implicit or explicit, of
creaturely acknowledgment of the transcendent. Such faith takes
shape in some set of religious or ideological *beliefs*, though it seems
for some people that a *pro forma* assent to a particular belief system
exists without an accompanying faith. That belief system is in turn
translated into *religious institutions* such as formulated doctrines,
sacred texts, life style, customs and laws, rituals, and community
structure. In any given instance these religious institutions may
flow more or less from faith and beliefs; ideally, the three elements
will be found together.

There seems to be no dispute that Jesus grew up in the hill country of Galilee in the town of Nazareth at a time of increasing crisis in the Palestinian Jewish community. For several centuries Jews had been faced with severe cultural challenges to their traditional beliefs in Yahweh as the transcendent guide and guardian of their history—from the Persian influence that touched them in their Babylonian exile, and for some time after the restoration of Jerusalem; then from the Ptolemaic and Seleucid kingdoms that ruled over them in the period after Alexander; then from the Romans, whose domination began with Pompey's campaign of 66 B.C.E. While the Roman presence was clearly in evidence in Jesus' day, it was Hellenistic culture that created the most severe test of Israel's identity and integrity as a religious community.

With the Babylonian exile, the cruder temptations to "paganism"—to participation in the vegetation cults of the surrounding religions that had marked Israel's history from the time of the Exodus right up to the Deuteronomic reform—faded from the picture. Instead, the subtler influences of Persian and Hellenistic secularization threatened the purity of Israel's faith at the very time that their religious reflection had finally arrived at genuine monotheism. Obviously, this threat was greater in the Diaspora where, as a minority, the Jewish population lived and worked and interacted with peoples whose beliefs were a mixture of cultural polytheism and practical agnosticism.

Until recently, students of the pre-Christian Near East tended to think of Palestinian Judaism as relatively untouched by this infiltration of Hellenistic thought and mores. However, the scholarly research of the last few decades, especially since Martin Hengel's *Judaism and Hellenism* (1974), has drawn attention to the extent of Hellenic influence on Palestinian Judaism.[2]

Some infiltration of Greek ideas and mores probably occurred before the second century B.C.E., but it was above all with the ascendancy (from about 200 B.C.E. onward) of Seleucid power in Palestine that the homeland of Judaism was faced with an aggressive campaign of Hellenization. Unlike what happened in most other parts of the Alexandrian conquest, where the Hellenistic overlay formed an easy syncretism with earlier religious beliefs, most Palestinian Jews resisted such a corruption of Yahwistic religion and denounced those Jews who sought an accommodation with the apparently more sophisticated culture of Greece. The result was that a notable division developed between "modernism" and "traditionalism" within Palestinian Judaism itself. With the attempts of Antiochus Epiphanes IV to impose religious and cultural practices offensive to the religious sensitivities of a large portion of the populace, the mounting tension erupted in the Maccabean revolt. The Maccabean successes and the influence of the Hasidim offset for a time the more obvious absorption of Hellenism into Jewish life, but the process of acculturation continued to divide Palestinian Jews into sharply opposed parties and sects right up to the destruction of Jerusalem in 70 C.E.

Jerusalem was logically the center of this ferment. It was at Jerusalem that the division between Sadducees, who espoused openness to the Hellenistic culture of the Mediterranean, and Pharisees, who fought for preservation of the "true faith," was most keenly felt, even within the Sanhedrin. It was in negative reaction to the worldliness of the Sadducean Temple establishment that the Essene communities isolated themselves from Judaism's public religious ritual in order—as they saw it—to preserve the purity of Israel's priesthood.

Galilee, however, was a separate and in significant ways different situation despite its allegiance to the law and its strong ties with the Temple; and it was its distinctive Jewish outlook and life that formed the context in which Jesus experienced the God he knew as Abba.[3] While one cannot discount a certain impact of Hellenistic culture on Jesus and his immediate disciples, it is the less urbanized Judaism of rural southern Galilee that provided the matrix for Jesus' experience of the divine and of himself in relation to the divine.

Galilee was separated from Judea by the hostile territory of the Samaritans. For the most part, Galilee's Jewish population was settled in villages whose way of life and world view were quite different from those of the few Hellenistic or Roman cities like

Sepphoris or Caesarea.[4] A word needs to be said about Sepphoris, however, because of its location—only a few miles from Nazareth—and because of its special role in the history of Jesus' day.[5]

Sepphoris had been, in the first century B.C.E., the most important city in Galilee with a Jewish population. In the wars between Herod and Antigonus (40-37 B.C.E.) it was an important garrison town, but in the revolt against Herod it was put to flames and its inhabitants sold into slavery. Rebuilt by Herod Antipas some years later and settled intentionally with a mixed populace—still predominantly Jewish but with distinctive Hellenistic cultural elements (theater, etc.)—it functioned off and on as the capital of Galilee and remained the strongest military fortress in the province. At the time of Jesus, Sepphoris seems to have been inhabited by an influential group of priestly aristocracy as well as Jewish craftsmen and merchants. The city's idiosyncratic character in the midst of the Galilean population was illustrated by the fact that in the insurrection prior to 70 C.E., the city sided with the Romans rather than with the rebels. Apparently this was a question of lacking sympathy for the revolutionary cause and not just a matter of self-preservation based on the judgment of the superior military strength of the Roman legions.[6]

Among the Jews living in the villages that dotted the countryside, there was probably an ambiguous attitude toward Hellenistic ideas and mores. While these villagers no doubt absorbed some of the atmosphere of Hellenistic and Roman city life, since they had to deal with such things as tax collection, sale of goods to city dwellers, and encounters with caravans and itinerant merchants, they nevertheless possessed a deep-seated suspicion of the "pagan" customs and "idolatrous" religious notions of both the non-Jews and the modernizing Jews. Because their village was situated within view of Sepphoris and close to the main road that linked Jerusalem and Sepphoris, the inhabitants of Nazareth could not have escaped acquaintance with and influence by these mixed cultural and politico-economic forces.

Prior to the Maccabean period, the territory of Galilee was peopled for the most part by non-Jews. Simon Maccabeus is described as gathering together the Jewish minority in the region bordering on Tyre and Sidon and bringing them to Judea for their own protection. With the success of the war against the Seleucids and the ascendancy of the Hasmoneans, the Galilean scene changed, particularly in the south. The populace was forced by Antigonus to convert to Jewish beliefs, or at least to the external ritual of circumcision, with the result that the population outside the cities became predominantly Jewish during the century before the birth of Jesus.[7] Though Galilee remained surrounded by non-Jewish peoples and the larger cities within Galilee were Hellenistic or Roman foundations, the Jews in Galilee kept their strong bonds with the Jews to the south, and especially with Jerusalem and its Temple.[8]

There is still little researched data that allows for a clear picture of Jewish religious life in a Galilean village like Nazareth. That the inhabitants of such a village were deeply attached to the law and to the Jerusalem Temple is clear, but the extent to which the Pharisaic interpretations of the law affected nonurban Galilee at the time of Jesus is difficult to determine. The traditions surrounding Yohanan ben Zakkai and his wonder-working disciple, Hanina ben Dosa, indicate that at least some Pharisaic teachers from Jerusalem were active in Galilee; but the lack of success that met Johanan indicates also that the Galileans were less than accepting of the Jerusalem teachers.[9] This would seem to suggest that Galilean villagers at the time of Jesus were neither strongly attracted to and influenced by the modernizing currents of Hellenized Judaism, nor deeply touched by the more sophisticated antimodernism of Pharisaic conservatism. Rather, theirs was a simple adherence to the Judaism to which much of the region had clung for at least as far back as Antigonus, a Judaism of the Torah and the Temple that was scribally but not Pharisaically interpreted.

As Jesus grew into adulthood, he would therefore have been basically influenced by this unquestioning acceptance of the religion of Israel as expressed in the Hebrew Bible. Still, the traditions about Jesus' public ministry reflect a person who was acquainted to a considerable extent with Pharisaic techniques of interpretation and with the later currents of Jewish wisdom literature, such as Sirach. Again, though there is a striking absence in the Gospels of any mention of Jesus relating to the city of Sepphoris, it is a bit difficult to imagine that a young craftsman growing up only ten kilometers from the city would never have frequented it to market his goods or out of sheer interest in visiting it—despite the basic distaste for the "decadence" of Hellenistic ways that probably was instilled in him by his local village and family ethos.

In his recent study of the economic situation of Galilee at the time of Jesus, Douglas Oakman proposes an interesting hypothesis about the activity of Jesus during his early adulthood.[10] Describing the itinerant character of many carpenters' employment in Palestine at the time of Jesus, and combining this with the indications in the Gospels that Jesus was well acquainted with some people in Judea before his preaching ministry brought him to Jerusalem, Oakman suggests that Jesus may well have spent time working in Judea or in Caesarea or perhaps earlier in Sepphoris. If this was so, and once one examines the evidence it does not seem implausible, this would have meant that for more than a decade before his public ministry Jesus would have attended synagogue in more urban situations and there become versed in Pharisaic explanation of the Torah. Intriguing as is Oakman's suggestion, and though it would, if true, help explain several enigmatic elements of the Gospel narratives, for the moment it must remain as interesting speculation. However, the basic picture of economic activity in Jesus' Palestine that Oakman provides does a great deal to flesh out the picture of the Palestinian culture that shaped Jesus' experience.

No matter what contacts Jesus in his years of residence in Galilee might have had with Hellenistic (or for that matter, Roman) thought or culture, it is highly probable that his culturally derived understanding of the divine was free from the syncretistic elements that touched the Sadducean aristocracy or even more the inhabitants of Samaria. Instead, it was the text of the Bible, no doubt explained within his family and in the local synagogue, that gave form to his religiously structured view of God. As Bernard Lee has emphasized in *The Galilean Jewishness of Jesus*, this meant that Jesus' understanding of God was not shaped in the essentialist categories characteristic of Greek philosophy. Rather, it was shaped by the distinctively "historical" God of Israelitic tradition—Yahweh who acts in history in dialectical interaction with human freedom, a God of love joined to justice, a God of mercy but also of punishment, not a God of abstract infinity and impassibility.[11] If one can read back into Jesus' formative years his understanding of God as reflected in the parables, it was above all the God proclaimed by the great Israelitic prophets that gave *form* to the "Abba experience" that remained for Jesus the controlling insight into the divine.

What this means is that the religious outlook of Jesus was *traditional* and *conservative* in the deepest sense of those two terms. At least as far as we can recover it from the Gospel texts, Jesus' understanding of the divinity he experienced as Abba preserved and deepened the mainstream currents of Israelite/Jewish belief.[12] For that very reason, however, it is difficult to relate him to religious currents of his day that might be thought of as "conservative." Pharisaism, for example, could be considered the conservative wing of Jewish thought in Jesus' day because it opposed the Hellenizing modernism of the Sadducees, espoused politically and socially the traditional claims to Jewish autonomy and distinctiveness, and laid basic stress on detailed observance of the law. At the same time, Pharisaism was basically a revolutionary reinterpretation of the law and of its role in the people's lives.

A superficial view of Jesus' public ministry has often, without qualification, contrasted Jesus' attitude toward Judaism with that of the Pharisees. However, whether one sees a causal link or explains it simply as a parallelism grounded in shared religious influences, there are striking similarities between the views of Jesus and those of the school of Hillel. Jesus' criticisms of Pharisaic points of view as reflected in the Gospels relate rather to the more rigid teaching of the school of Shammai. Still, there is enough precedent in the prophetic literature, in the Eighteen Benedictions, and in the Psalms to explain Jesus' and Hillel's "mild" view of God that one does not have to attribute any direct Pharisaic influence on Jesus. One of the unknown factors in making a judgment is the extent to which Jesus traveled, lived, or worked in Judea prior to his two or three years of public prophetic ministry.[13]

On a key issue, central to Jesus' teaching and to that of the school of Hillel, namely, the sanctification of "ordinary" life, there is a deceptive appearance of similarity but actually a radical difference. Both see the noncultic activity of humans as the arena of encounter with God; but Pharisaism sees this happening through the importation of sacerdotal sacralization into this daily life, whereas Jesus' teaching underscores the holiness intrinsic to human life in itself. Ben Meyer has made a convincing case for the fact that Jesus was conscious of starting something new, even if this awareness remained unspecified as to institutionalized details.[14] And it would seem that this "something new" he felt himself initiating had to do precisely with the saving presence of God working through the nonformally religious elements of people's lives.[15]

That Jesus' aim to bring into being "a new thing" remained so unstructured leads to an important difference between this book's study of Jesus' religious experience and most others, including the recent essays of Bernard Lee and Ed Sanders.[16] While most studies focus on Jesus' experience of *institutionalized religion*, that is, his conscious participation in the various aspects of Jewish religious practice, the focus of the present study is on Jesus' experience of God. Admittedly, this is much more difficult to discover from the evidences we have, and it can be reached for the most part only through Jesus' involvement with the Judaism of his day. However, to the extent that one can legitimately extrapolate from the external religious behavior of Jesus to his internal awareness of the transcendent he knew as Abba, to that extent one has a perspective from which to understand better the source of Jesus' profound "discontent" with the Jewish religion he so deeply cherished.

Justification for this concentration of Jesus' experience of *God* seems clear from Jesus' own teaching and from the first two decades of Christianity's emergence after his death. There is no indication that Jesus ever prescribed formally religious behavior other than that already practiced by people. If he did deal with religious practice at all, it was only to insist on the internal attitudes from which authentic religious actions should proceed. On the other hand, his teaching, which reflected his own interests and inner attitudes, dealt constantly with the character of his Abba. What was revolutionary and revelatory about Jesus' experience was not primarily his experience of religion (that is, the institutionalizing of Jewish belief and piety through doctrinal formulations, rituals, legal prescriptions, etc.), but his experience of God which, of course, did radically transform his experience of religion at the same time that it did not fit it. While his self-identification as eschatological prophet, as we will see, occurred within the framework of established Judaism, it came from his awareness of relatedness to his Abba and of doing Abba's will and not from situating himself within the structures of the Judaism of his day. Most radically, it was the "difference" of the God he knew that brought him into ultimate conflict with the religious leadership of his day.

In summary, and arguing chiefly from the understandings and attitudes and goals that underpinned his public career, one can see that Jesus in his years of growth toward maturity was influenced neither by Greek ideas in his understanding of the divine, nor by Hellenistic cultural elements in his practice of religion. Rather, he was thoroughly Jewish in the formation received at home, in his education from the synagogue, in his relation to Jerusalem and its Temple.

But Jewish in what way? For Jesus' contemporaries were deeply split over what it meant to be truly Jewish. There is no trace of anti-Jewish feeling in Jesus' public teaching, and to that extent one could say that he was patriotically Jewish. On the other hand, he was not narrowly nationalistic, and he was not sympathetic to the violent position often attributed to the Zealots.[17] The key to Jesus' attitude toward the political situation of his day was his trust that in some fashion his Father would honor the promises made to

[handwritten: Jesus distinguished between Abba + faithfulness And the Jewish religious institutions]

Israel over the centuries. A basic rejection of Judaism would not have seemed compatible with what he knew of Abba. Instead, he would most likely have shared with most of his Jewish contemporaries an expectation that the resoration of Jerusalem and its Temple that began with the return from Babylonian exile would reach a fuller and final expression. However, as we will see, this apparently did not guarantee for him the absoluteness of Jewish *religious institutions* as they then existed.[18]

A closer look at three key agents of Jesus' religious formation can flesh out the description of the developing view of the divine and of himself in relationship to the divine that was central to his growth into maturity: (1) his home life in Nazareth, (2) his education through the synagogue, and (3) his participation in the liturgies of the Jerusalem Temple.

1. *Home.* For the young Jesus growing through childhood into maturity, what would have been the experience of God and of the religious expressions of his and his extended family's relationship to this God? Perhaps the first and most important thing to insist upon is that any separation of Jesus' religious experience from the remainder of his daily human experience is artificial and incompatible with the realities of his life in Nazareth. In a way and to an extent that is difficult for people today to appreciate, the entirety of daily experience was for the inhabitants of early first-century Nazareth "lived with" the God of Israel.

The texts of the New Testament give us precious little about the Nazareth situation, but a couple of incidental remarks suggest that the family of Jesus was devotedly Jewish, with the daily routine of their little village revolving around the local synagogue and with the pilgrimage to Jerusalem and the Temple providing the high point of each year. Remembering that Nazareth was a small and poor village, perhaps numbering little more than fifteen hundred people, we can surmise that their existence was almost that of an extended family for whom the synagogue, anything but an imposing religious structure, would have functioned naturally as their one gathering place. Thus we can presume that the prescribed daily practices of Judaism would have been the taken-for-granted pattern of their life. As far as we can gather, Nazareth at the time of Jesus would not yet have seen the Pharisees' transfer of priestly/Temple cultic purity to daily life; instead, human existence as such was assumed to be given by God as good and in no particular need of being "sanctified." Blessings attached to the normal things of life, but only in the sense that God was blessed for having provided food and drink, light and rest, and all that was good and life-sustaining.

Historical and archaeological evidence indicates that Nazareth's economy, like that of other villages in lower Galilee, was essentially based on agriculture, which meant that most of its inhabitants were engaged in raising crops for their own food, for offerings to the Temple and tithes to the priests, and perhaps for market in nearby Sepphoris. Jesus' family, then, would have had that proximity to the soil and that sense of dependence upon sun and rain and weather which characterizes agrarian groups. For them, that would have meant a constant sense of their dependence upon Yahweh blessing them with favorable conditions for their harvests and gratitude for the harvests when they were bountiful. This would have been reinforced by the agricultural character of the great Temple feasts.[19] Even though Jesus as a craftsman would have been engaged otherwise than in farming, he would have constantly shared the interests and worries and gratifications of his fellow villagers, been part of their daily conversations about their farming, and probably spent much of his time providing tools, etc., for their work. This is reflected in the prominence of agricultural metaphors in his parables.

From the recitation of the Shema and accompanying benedictions as soon as one arose in the morning to its repetition with other benedictions before retiring at day's end, the day was filled with reminders of divine providential presence.[20] Blessings would have been attached to the morning and evening meals, and very likely (as suggested by Dan. 6:11) the prescription of prayer three times during the day was already in effect.[21] The day's routine was not a monastic one, since for most of the prayer there was no question of leaving work situations in order to gather in "sacred space";

daily prayer

rather, it resembled rural life in many Catholic areas of Europe where, until recently, people responded to the Angelus bells wherever they were and whatever they were doing at the moment, or was like the response in Muslim lands to the cry of the muezzein. However, it is possible that occasionally at day's end the villagers of Nazareth would have gathered in the synagogue for the recitation of the Shema and benedictions.

Though it is impossible to know the exact formulation of the prayers then in use, we can know with high probability the general content and the overall mentality they expressed. As for the Shema, which was actually a profession of faith rather than a prayer as such, we do know its exact form because it consisted in two passages from Deuteronomy (6:4-9, 11:13-21) and one from Numbers (15:37-41).

In reciting twice daily the prescribed Shema, Jesus would have experienced being a member of a believing community—the immediate group to which he belonged, and beyond that, the Jewish people including past generations of Israel. Inseparable from this awareness of sharing Jewish faith would have been the awareness that the words "Hear, O Israel, the Lord your God . . ." dealt with the transcendent divinity of whom he was always conscious. Thus his pervading consciousness of the transcendent was being shaped daily by the theistic, indeed monotheistic, formulations of Jewish belief.

Several aspects of the Shema can be identified as modeling forces in Jesus' experience of the divine. Clearly, the God of whom Jesus is conscious as his Abba is, in the Shema, described as the personal ruler of all reality, "the Lord," the God who picked Moses to lead Israel and who entrusted the law to Moses as norm for the chosen people. For Jewish faithful, "the Lord" was the guide of their destiny, leading them by his law, which was the path to life. Drawing from its Deuteronomic source, the Shema placed both the giving and the reception of the law in the context of love.

The response of each faithful Jew comes in observance of this law, but such observance is grounded in the overarching requirement—you shall *love* the Lord your God. This would have resonated in Jesus with his emerging sense of being loved by his Abba. In addition, it would have set up a special sensitivity to the prophetic view of Israel's God because the Deuteronomic reorientation of the law by the command of love is, if not derived from the prophetic currents associated with Hosea and Jeremiah, at least closely linked with them in spirit.[22]

The divinity envisaged by the Shema is a God of history, the protector and guide of Israel from the Exodus to eschatological fulfillment, the creator and ruler of the universe, the one and only true God, a personal divinity who communicates with humans, directs their lives, and cares for them with gentle power. Thus would Jesus' structured understanding of his Abba have been shaped by his Jewish beliefs.

The benedictions accompanying the Shema were praises directed to the Abba Jesus knew—expressions of gratitude for gifts of life and blessing, expressions of trust in a caring but just God who, though merciful, was unaccepting of evil in any form. Sunrise and sunset were natural occasions for such benedictions; so also were the meals which were seen as God's provision for the life of his people. Jesus' awareness of his Abba was, as far as we can reconstruct it from the prevailing Galilean culture, a continuous response of gratitude for the daily experiences lived in the consciousness of God's guiding and supporting presence.

Each week this daily routine found intensified form in the Sabbath. At home the meals were marked with extra blessings, particularly the Kiddush, and the proscription of physical labor accentuated the dedication of the day to special awareness of the divine presence. Though commemorative of God's mercy to Israel, this implicitly placed people's daily life in a future-oriented context. The Sabbath was a special "family day"; at the same time, it found its religious focus in the synagogue where much of the day was spent.

Since Hanukkah and Purim were not occasions for pilgrimage to Jerusalem, the villagers of Nazareth would no doubt have celebrated them in home and synagogue. This would have meant that young Nazarenes like Jesus would have grown up with the legendary accounts of religious heroism (the Maccabees and Esther).[23] More importantly, they would have grown up with the view that God protects and vindicates "the just" and overcomes Israel's enemies. Hanukkah in particular would have reinforced the expectations of restoration that were prevalent in Jesus' day.[24]

2. Synagogue. In trying to reconstruct the role of the synagogue in the experience of Jesus, it is important to remain aware of the broad function of this institution in the life of a village like Nazareth or Capernaum. Our tendency is to think of the synagogue rather exclusively as a place of worship, supplementing the Jerusalem Temple and for many in the Diaspora a "stand-in" for the Temple. However, the synagogue was basically a place of meeting, above all for learning and reflecting upon the Torah. Actually, such pondering on the Torah came increasingly to be seen as the very heart of worship.[25]

Very often an elementary school, attended by boys between ages seven and thirteen, was connected with the synagogue; and in urban centers, above all in Jerusalem, a school for more advanced study would help prepare those who would later perform professional roles as experts in the Torah.[26] Even for those who had no such professional ambitions, learning extended into adult life; Jewish men came together to ponder and discuss the law, often in the synagogue though not exclusively there. The synagogue was also the common place for other public gatherings and for prayer— certainly on the Sabbath, but often for daily evening devotions.

It is probable that Jesus, as a young Jewish male, would have been schooled at the tiny Nazareth synagogue, instructed in the lore and life of his people by the local schoolmaster/scribe who would build upon the knowledge being imparted in the home. Since Nazareth did have a synagogue, in all likelihood with a *hazzan* to assist the head of the synagogue, and since it was the *hazzan* who generally served as the schoolteacher, there is a good chance that Jesus did enjoy such elementary education.[27] Reading was taught, and no doubt also some Hebrew, so that as adults they could read the scrolls in the synagogue; instruction was given in the history and beliefs and ethical prescriptions of Jewish tradition, and there was perhaps also some instruction in writing (the Gospel scene of Jesus with the woman taken in adultery presumes that Jesus knew how to write).[28] Basically, the purpose of the education was to provide enough knowledge about the conduct of Jewish life and worship so that the pupil could later function as a devout Jew in home and synagogue. The only textbook for instruction was the Hebrew Bible itself—not too limiting a choice, since it was an anthology of more than a millennium of Israelitic culture. It is unlikely that in these early years Jesus would have had any exposure to pseudepigraphical literature, though some of the notions prevalent in such literature may well have been "in the air" and been incidentally communicated by the synagogue teacher.

Naturally, one wonders about the interpretation of the Bible that would have been given Galilean boys at the time of Jesus. The father of the family was the one primarily charged with instruction about the Bible; he, in turn, would have been instructed by his father. But this was most likely supplemented by other teaching—at the time of Jesus by the *hazzan* in the synagogue school. Who would this teacher have been and where would he himself have received the knowledge he imparted to his young charges? One is tempted to respond in terms of the developing Pharisaic influence on the teaching connected with Jewish synagogues. And it is true that in general the doctrinal perspective of Jesus in his public teaching is more consonant with Pharisaism than with any other sect at the time.[29] The problem with the hypothesis of Pharisaic influence on Jesus' early education is the evidence that points to *minimal* Pharisaic influence in Galilean synagogues at the time of Jesus.

One of the puzzling questions about Jesus' earlier life is how he became acquainted with the more technical ways of dealing with scriptural texts, a skill he manifested in his public career. His command of Pharisaic methods of interpretation was such that a few modern historians think that Jesus may himself have belonged to the Pharisees and that his criticisms of some aspects of Pharisaism was a criticism from within the movement.[30] However, there is little to substantiate this view; indeed, it seems rather clear that Jesus was not a *Pharisaic* teacher—his manner was more direct, "he teaches as one with authority."[31] Certainly in his mature years Jesus would have been exposed to the Sabbath reading and sermon in synagogues outside Nazareth; in addition, he would have had opportunity over the years to hear the scribal teaching in Jerusalem when he came to share in the Temple liturgies. By themselves, however, these do not seem sufficient to explain the acquaintance with Pharisaic teaching that Jesus manifested in his disputes with "the scribes and Pharisees."[32]

The synagogue was not only a place for instruction of the young and the place where the village men would gather to reflect together on the Torah and to discuss and perhaps settle the arrangements of local life; it was preeminently the place where they prayed as a community. As we already suggested, in a small village like Nazareth some people may have gathered each evening to recite the Shema and two or three accompanying benedictions; but certainly the villagers came together on the Sabbath to acknowledge the God of Israel by reading and reflecting on the sacred texts and by prayer.[33]

Though the heart of the Sabbath synagogue service was the reading of and reflection on the sacred texts, there was also the recitation of prayers.[34] Probably the most important prayer consisted of the recitation of the *Shemoneh Esreh*, the Eighteen Benedictions. The evidence is clear, by the second century, that the Eighteen Benedictions in prescribed form were a central element in the synagogue Sabbath service. It is not certain that these benedictions antedated the destruction of the Jerusalem Temple and, if they did, whether the formulations contained in rabbinic traditions were already in use. However, as Safrai points out, "All of them (the Talmudic traditions) reflect the feeling that the fixed framework of the Eighteen Benedictions already existed to some extent during the last generations of the Second Temple."[35] From early on in rabbinic Judaism, these benedictions were to be recited three times a day by every Jew, including women, slaves, and children. There is no clear evidence, however, that this practice was already in force at the time of Jesus. Nevertheless, the close resemblance of the canonical text of the Benedictions (from the post-70 C.E. period) to Sirach 51 supports the contention that already in the second century B.C.E. the benedictions, in a form quite close to the later prescribed text, were a key element of both private and synagogue prayer.[36] So we are on solid ground in arguing to Jesus' experience of prayer in the synagogue from the content of the Eighteen Benedictions as we know them from rabbinic sources.

Most importantly, these prayers were *benedictions*. Like the daily benedictions accompanying the Shema and like the grace at meals in the home, these prayers were a grateful acknowledgment of God's blessings on his people. Throughout the blessings there is recognition of the universal rule of Yahweh; "king" is a repeated title, always with the implication of "benevolent ruler." Again, the title "Father" is found in two of the benedictions. "Lord, our God" is the most frequent title, and it is clear that "Lord of history" as well as "Lord of creation" is implied, for Yahweh is blessed as "God of our fathers," as "redeemer of Israel," "mighty, powerful, and eternal," "holy and awesome," yet compassionate and accepting of a repentant Israel. Yahweh is a God who works in the hearts of people, turning them from sin and comforting them in their grief, granting them the gift of understanding the law. Yahweh is a God who frees and protects his people from enemies, cosmic and human; a God, finally, who bestows blessings on his faithful ones.

Such a view of Israel's God, reiterated daily in the prayers that made up the rhythm of Jesus' consciousness as he grew into adulthood, would have resonated without conflict with the intimate and immediate experience he had of this divinity, his Abba. However, it would have interpreted that immediate experience of the transcendent in terms of the particular cultural categories and imagery that made up Jewish belief. Probably the lack of "cognitive dissonance" between his own distinctive awareness and the religious understandings of his Galilean upbringing was aided by the relative lack of an official (and therefore limiting) interpretation provided by trained theologians.

Did he also, through the synagogue, acquire some knowledge of late wisdom literature or of apocalyptic writings such as the Books of Enoch, the Testament of Moses, or the Book of Jubilees, or of prayers like the Psalms of Solomon? There is no way of knowing, but it is unlikely that he would have been exposed to such literature in the years before leaving Nazareth. Still, there are Gospel texts—such as Matthew 11—which, to the extent that they are traceable to Jesus himself, reflect more than passing acquaintance with books like Sirach. The case of Sirach is particularly tantalizing, because the discovery of a Hebrew text of Sirach among the archaeological remains at Masada suggests a rather wide circulation of that book as a semicanonical text at the time of Jesus.

3. *The Jerusalem Temple.* In his recent book, *Jesus and Judaism*, E.P. Sanders takes as the verifiable historical happening on which to base his study of Jesus the "cleansing of the Temple" that is narrated or alluded to in all of the Gospel traditions. Whatever the exact occurrence—Sanders reads it much more as a symbolic threat of destruction of the then-existent Temple establishment than as a "cleansing"—it was this (in Sanders's view) that crystallized the hatred of the Temple high priesthood and triggered its resolve to eliminate Jesus from the scene.[37]

Without analyzing or appraising the case that Sanders makes for this scene as the key to why Jesus was put to death through the combined activity of the high priests and the Roman authorities, it is clear that the Temple played a distinctive role in the last phase of Jesus' public ministry. Very likely, then, the experiences he had in the Temple were a major contributing factor to the overall religious experience of Jesus of Nazareth and, most importantly, to the tensions that developed in that experience during his public ministry.

As we saw, Galilean Jews were strongly attached to the Temple and participated regularly in its great liturgical festivities. This probably would have been truer for residents of Nazareth because of its location near the southern border of Galilee and therefore its greater identification with what took place in Judea. It is all but certain that Jesus, during the years of his growth into maturity and then as an adult Jewish male, shared regularly in the major Temple feasts. Moreover, religiously he would have identified with Jerusalem and its Temple as the "holy city," the place of his Abba's special dwelling with his people and of that people's most cherished and most effective cultic activity. For Jews, there was only the one Temple, and all Jewish worship, even in the synagogues of the Diaspora, was oriented geographically toward that Temple.

So what would Jesus have experienced in relationship to this holiest of places?[38] An irreplaceable guide in answering this question is provided by the Bible's collection of Psalms, the hymnal of the Second Temple. The Psalms preserve for us the religious understandings and attitudes of Israelitic worshipers over the centuries and specifically of Jewish participants in the Temple liturgies at the time of Jesus; for these hymns verbalize the people's response to the "word" they received in the proclamation of the law and the performance of Temple ritual.[39]

For Jews who came to the Temple from a distance, as did those from Galilee, the religious experience of the great feasts began with the pilgrimage to Jerusalem; and the "Psalms of ascent" give us some notion of the excitement and expectation with which they approached the city. Psalm 122, for example, voiced the joy of the group as they undertook the journey—"the joy I felt when they said to me, 'Let us go to the house of the Lord'"—and the prayer that peace would reign in the holy city. Identifying themselves with the "little ones," they come to their God seeking loving acceptance rather than the rejection they so often experience from the haughty and powerful (Psalm 123). As one adverts to this pilgrimage experience, it is interesting to reflect on the different religious mentality of the Galileans as pilgrims and the Jews in and around Jerusalem who did not have this experience and who felt themselves in possession of the religious center.

Once in Jerusalem, the pilgrims were part of the festive occurrences that marked the holy days. Indications are that rules about diet and apparel were not as strictly interpreted during the festive times—a concession to "outsiders" who would not be accustomed to the more stringent observance that otherwise prevailed, and a measure to foster mingling among people from various localities. Thus for the growing Jesus, the God who was the focus of the pilgrimage was clearly one who wished joy for his chosen people— the Temple liturgies themselves would have been essentially times of cultic rejoicing, rituals in which dance and song and musical accompaniment were appropriately integrated with the priestly actions in the sanctuary. One can easily imagine Jesus in his youthful years, as well as later, joining with the men as they danced throughout "the night of Tabernacles" in the court of the women, or sharing in the pilgrims' procession as they marched around the altar waving their willow branches.

Devout Jews attending these Temple rituals (and Jesus would have been among these) would observe the recognition of Yahweh's sovereignty through the sacrificial oblation of the victims and through the libations poured at the base of the altar, would petition their God for continuing protection and blessing, and would pledge themselves to faithful fulfillment of the covenant through observance of the law. In response to the priestly blowing of the trumpets, they would have prostrated themselves in worship of Yahweh, the God of their ancestors; and they would have joined in the refrains so often repeated in the Psalms, "for his mercy endures forever . . ." What went through their minds as the various elements of the liturgy unfolded is reflected in the Psalms that either accompanied or responded to the liturgical actions.

Central to the liturgy of the Temple were the regular morning and evening whole burnt offerings. Even on the great festivals, these provided generally in somewhat amplified form the essential act of worship. Flanked by a Levite and a representative of the lay delegation, the officiating priest would hold aloft the carcass of the sacrificial animal and then place it on the altar to be consumed by the fire. Meanwhile there was the singing of Psalms led by the Levites, often antiphonally arranged so that the people could join (for example, Psalms 146-150), and prostrations by the people at appropriate moments.

44

As one peruses the Psalms prescribed for each day, one encounters the main themes of Israel's history and Temple worship. Psalm 24, on the first day of the week, recalls David's bringing the ark into Jerusalem and acclaims Yahweh as king of glory entering *his* city. On the next two days, Psalm 48 and Psalm 82 recognize Yahweh as Israel's savior, conquering enemies and false gods and unjust judges within. At midweek, Psalm 74 calls on God to fight against the profaners of the Temple. The next day, Psalm 81 (used also in Tabernacles) describes the God of the covenant appealing to the people as their savior. And on the vigil of the Sabbath, Psalm 93 praises Yahweh as creator whose law governs all things. Finally, on the Sabbath itself, during the wine libation, Psalm 92 celebrates Yahweh's love and protection of the just.[40]

Three basic themes ran through all the Temple liturgies: grateful praise of God for the blessings of creation and covenant and for his fidelity to his promises, recognition of the Temple's holiness as Yahweh's dwelling place, and loving acceptance and faithful observance of Yahweh's law (Psalms 95, 96, 122, 132, 135). Perhaps nothing provided a more triumphant expression of Jewish faith in their God than the great chant of the Hallel (Psalms 113-118).[41] Almost as solemn as the moment of animal sacrifice was the pouring of the libation of wine or, on the Feast of Tabernacles, of water. This, too, was accompanied by Levites singing, by musical instruments, and by the blowing of the trumpets—the signal for the people to prostrate themselves in adoration.

One of the features of Temple service in its later stages was an emphasis on proclamation and explanation of the law. Every seventh year the king himself was to read the Torah on the Feast of Tabernacles; but the ordinary routine found the Torah proclaimed on all festivals and even on regular Sabbaths. This was, of course, in addition to the readings of and reflections on Torah that were constantly taking place throughout the Temple compound.

No Psalm pays lengthier tribute to the people's devotion to the law than Psalm 119, which was part of the liturgy for Tabernacles. Probably soon after the solemn entry procession into the Temple courts, the high priest proclaimed a portion of the law—

reminiscent of Ezra's action in the rededication of the Temple (as narrated in Nehemiah 8), and the assembly would then break into the lengthy praise of the law and commitment to its observance. If this lengthy Psalm, each portion announced by a letter of the alphabet, expressed the people's commitment to the law, it also expressed their view of the divine lawgiver. Though the fact that the law was *law* unavoidably carried implications of divine will sanctioned by reward or punishment, Psalm 119 reflects the Jewish view of a God who is not dominating but guiding, a law that is not restriction but a path, a law that is blessing rather than burden.

At the close of the liturgy the priests would gather together on the steps of the sanctuary, where they could be seen by the people through the Nicanor gate, and invoked the blessing of God upon the assembly.

If the regular rhythms of Temple worship provided these elements of Jesus' religious experience, the great festivals had their own intensified and distinctive communication of one or other of these major themes. Tabernacles is an especially intriguing instance because of the numerous resonances with its liturgy in the New Testament texts.[43] Celebration of the feast during Jesus' lifetime would have kept alive the memory of restoration already partially accomplished and hope for its fulfillment. "Restoration" was in the air in Jesus' day; carrying it to its eschatological realization seems to have been the dominant element in Jesus' awareness of his prophetic mission.[44] So while there would be no way of weighing the influence of this Temple feast on Jesus' awareness of his Abba, its liturgy would certainly have been consonant with and reinforcing of the other elements of his religious experience that we can discern.

It is interesting to speculate about the precise activity of Jesus during his participation in Temple worship, but it can be little more than speculation. Any involvement in the official actions of the priesthood is easily ruled out, because he certainly did not belong to a priestly family; his participation in the Temple liturgies would have been that of the ordinary lay person. Even the limited prominence he gained during his short public career meant no

Jesus prophetic experience (Abba) made his experience of the Temple priesthood + institution one of dis-content!

increased role in the Temple liturgies, though it might have enlarged his audience as he, among many others, taught in the outer Temple court. The priestly reaction to his "cleansing" of the Temple makes it clear that he was considered by the official establishment as an outsider who was unjustifiably interfering in what was not his business. That he himself obviously did think it was his business appears to have stemmed from his Abba experience; the Temple was "his Father's house" and Jesus' devotion to the Temple was but a reflection of his devotion to his Abba.

For Jesus, then, the various elements of Temple worship in which he participated by attention, listening, song, and bodily movement served to translate into Jewish cultural terms the hearing and responding to the presence of his Abba that was the constant rhythm of his human experience. Basically these ritual forms resonated constantly with that experience, but as his relationship to the Temple priesthood became intensified and he became more aware of the actual aims and behavior of the inner circles of that priesthood, his discontent with the religious insincerity he observed led him increasingly to question the very institution itself.

This leads us, then, to a decisive question about Jesus' experience of the divine and its relationship to the Jewish cultural forms (language, ritual, life style) in which it was formulated and expressed: How absolute did he consider these Jewish forms to be? Obviously, the question was not unique to Jesus; in one way or another it is endemic to any prophetic experience that occurs within the context of a religion that claims to be grounded in historical revelation. However, it is correlative to the depth of that prophetic experience, and the immediacy of Jesus' exposure to the divine would have made the dilemma of consonance/dissonance especially acute.

At least as much as any believing Israelite, Jesus would have accepted the reality of God's intervention in the history of his people and seen such divine activity as "for real." His own Abba experience testified to the divine fidelity; therefore it was inconceivable that Yahweh, the God of his people, would not be faithful to his promises—specifically the promises made to Moses and David and Solomon and reiterated to the great charismatic prophets, the promises verbalized in the biblical texts used in synagogue and Temple. In some sense, the law and the Temple and even the kingship had to have a lasting role in the kingdom of God; but in ways not yet apparent, this role had to give way or be transformed by what God's Spirit was working in Jesus as the prophetic agent of eschatological establishment of the kingdom— this seems to have been the experience of Jesus as the crisis of conflict with the official establishment deepened. In conflict were Jesus' experience of God and his experience of religious institutions; Jesus remained faithful to his Abba, though this meant death amid alienation from all he had most cherished as a Jew.

= death + alienation

annotation at top: ✱ the structuring of his consciousness {categories of his thinking + images that shaped his awareness}

including his religious experience

took place within a strongly Patriarchal context

3

JESUS AS JEWISH MALE

Jesus' human experience was that of a Jew in first-century Galilee, but more specifically it was that of a Galilean *male*. Apart from the value intrinsic to discovering what elements of experience were proper to him precisely because he was a man living in a strongly patriarchal society, there is added impetus to determine exactly what this meant for him because of the "problem" about Jesus' masculinity that has been raised by Christian feminists in the last two decades. Briefly, once the distinctiveness of women's religious experience and the equal standing of that experience as "word of God" are accepted, there arises inevitably the question about the manner in which the male experience of Jesus can serve as a model for the Christian faith of women. This chapter makes no pretense of responding directly to that question; rather, its purpose is to clarify as far as possible what difference Jesus' masculinity made to his awareness of the transcendent and of his relation to that transcendent. This may in turn suggest some directions for dealing with the question as to whether women can relate to a male savior figure.[1]

As we have seen, Jesus was thoroughly Jewish. The categories of thinking and the images that shaped his awareness of self, the world, and God were those of his culture, even if they were profoundly challenged by the immediacy of his exposure to the divine. This meant that the structuring of his consciousness, in- ✱ cluding his religious experience, took place within a strongly patriarchal context.

The more obvious expression of this patriarchal tonality of his religious experience had to do with the language, especially the

49

metaphors, used by Jews of his day to think and talk about the divine. There is no need to expand on the statement that this language was thoroughly masculine; Yahweh, the God of Israel, was unquestionably *he*. He was the Lord, the king of the universe and of his people, the warrior/protector of his chosen Israel, the father of the children of Israel.[2] In the application of the marriage symbolism to Yahweh and the people, there could be no question but that his was the role of husband.[3] True, there are a few instances (for example, Isa. 49:15; Jer. 31:20) of feminine metaphors used by the prophets to describe Yahweh's mercy and loving care; but these are more than balanced by the misogyny implicit in the bitter denunciation of Israel's infidelity through use of the metaphor of wifely adultery.[4] Beautiful as is the portrayal of Yahweh's undying love and unquestioning forgiveness that one finds in Hosea or Jeremiah, Yahweh is nevertheless the betrayed husband; and it is the image of a faithless woman's lust that is used to illustrate the heinousness of Israel's sin (Ezekiel 16).

To some extent, the distortion involved in this use of the faithless woman as symbol of human sin can be met by pointing to the deeper realization—even in ancient Israelitic thought—that the reality of the divine transcends any such attempts to apply gender designation,[5] and by pointing to the Gospel's clear reference to the fidelity of Jesus' *women* disciples in the moment of crisis. However, the patriarchal character of the Jewish understanding of God at the time of Jesus goes deeper than the explicit verbal references to God as "he," or to the predominant use of masculine metaphors to provide some understanding of this God.

For Israelitic theology God, Yahweh was male *on principle*.[6] Leaving aside the disputed contentions that in its most primitive stage Israelitic religion worshiped a consort of Yahweh,[7] the "official" faith of Israel as enshrined in the canonical literature of the Hebrew Bible leaves no room for a female divinity parallel to or accompanying or in addition to "the God who led our ancestors out of Egypt."[8] The goddesses of the surrounding religions were unacceptable precisely because they stood for the autonomous forces of fertility that were the alternative to the providential omnipotence of Yahweh.[9] Certainly by the time that the priestly theology had crystallized in the description of creation that opens Genesis, the God of Israel is seen as one whose activity is purely imperial, with no hint of sexual activity; he simply commands, "Let there be light." Even the earlier Yahwistic version metaphorically describes the creator as "a craftsman," without any suggestion of mother earth being a coprinciple in the emergence of living beings.[10]

By the time of Jesus, this distancing of Yahweh from the fertility religions of the ancient Near East had long been established by the breakthrough monotheism reflected in Deutero Isaiah (Isaiah 45). Any mention of a female divinity was clear evidence that one was dealing with an idolatrous and "pagan" religion, not with the traditional faith of Israel. Actually, attempts at the accommodation of Jewish belief to Greek thought that took place in Hellenizing circles of Judaism in the two centuries prior to the time of Jesus reinforced the patriarchal implications of Judaism's God. The tendency was to identify Yahweh with Zeus, with the latter understood not as a particular divinity in the classical pantheon, but by "philosophical monotheism" as naming divinity as such.[11]

The very foundations of Israeliltic and then Jewish society were linked with the male metaphor for the divine. Behind the patriarchal structures of law and social arrangement and exercise of power by those in authority—beginning with the husband/father in the family—lay the law of Yahweh given to Moses. The completely patriarchal orientation of this law, which governed the least actions of the Jewish people, was beyond question; it was the expression of God's will. And Yahweh himself was the abiding enforcer of the Mosaic dispensation; he was the superpatriarch whose power and justice were imaged in the just earthly ruler (Psalm 97-99; 111).

One can go still deeper, however, into the patriarchal presumption of Yahweh's masculinity in the Judaism of Jesus' day. By Jesus' day, under scribal and especially Pharisaic influence, the most important focus of Jewish religious practice was reflection upon the Torah. Jewish males gathered at almost any occasion to read

God thinks the WAY men think.

together the law and reflect upon its meaning for life.[12] This ongoing Torah—for Torah was more than "the book"—constituted a continuing conversation between Yahweh and the people, that is, the men, for women were not included in this pursuit of insight into the Torah. When the people gathered at the synagogue on the Sabbath—and this included the women who listened and prayed, but did not share in comment on the law[13]—the very heart of the worship consisted in this reading and reflection.

If one examines this procedure, one can see the implicit notion that God to some extent thinks the way the human conversation partners do; otherwise these latter could have no notion of the divine "reasoning process" and there could be no conversation. However, these human dialoguers with God are *the men*. Their masculine way of thinking, both intrinsic and inherited by training, is the taken-for-granted model for God's way of thinking. God obviously thinks the way that men think, arranges things providentially the way that a practically minded man would do, exercises authority the way that Jewish fathers are meant to do, and in general exhibits those qualities that one would expect from the wise and powerful ruler of the universe and of human history.[14] Knowing how men would do things—just and wise men, of course—provides insight into how Yahweh wishes things to be done in accordance with the Torah.

Any Jewish male, including Jesus of Nazareth, would therefore have implicitly assumed that his own masculine experience of human awareness imaged divine consciousness and activity. Not that he would have formally thought about that, but the daily use of religious language about the divine and the verbal/symbolic import of the Jewish life of which he was a part placed him constantly in the context of patriarchal assumption. Moreover, the entire approach to authority in society to which Jesus was exposed and which formed part of his everyday existence, beginning with his own relationship to Joseph and extending to the religious and civil officials of his day, was grounded in a notion of societal power modeled by "father."

Jesus' very experience of being Jewish, of being a member of Israel, was inseparable from his being male; for it was only because he was a male that he could function as a full member of the chosen people. While the odious prayer formula used by Jewish males, "I thank you, God, that I was not born a gentile or a woman," came into usage somewhat later than Jesus' lifetime, the very structures of Jewish religious life reflected the judgment upon women as inferior, as incapable of Jewish identity on their own.[15] A striking symbol of this situation was the arrangement of the Jerusalem Temple where the women were relegated to their own area, which was further removed from the Holy of Holies than was the court of the men.

One of the most insidious aspects of this patriarchal situation was the accompanying notion that all of this was by divine institution. After all, it was the law that dictated these patterns and procedures for Jewish life, and the law had come from Yahweh himself through Moses. There could be, then, no injustice in this natural state of affairs. Or perhaps "natural" is not the appropriate word, for the biblical account of the Fall suggested that woman's secondary status was the result of Eve's sin in Eden; that in an unblemished humanity there might not be this dominance of the male over the female. In any event, the origin of Israel's social arrangements in Yahweh's own wisdom and decree apparently left no room for disagreeing with the patriarchal structuring of Jewish life.

Reconstructing this cultural context of Jesus' male consciousness creates some puzzling questions as one reflects on the activity of Jesus in his public ministry and on the attitudes underlying that activity. The Gospel texts as we have them do not draw attention to the relationship of Jesus to women, but the recent application of feminist hermeneutic to the New Testament has revealed, "between the lines," a reflection of the somewhat scandalous attitude of Jesus toward women.[16] By the time the New Testament texts crystallized, the prominence of women in the circle of Jesus' disciples was already being obscured. One almost senses a certain embarrassment as the evangelists find it difficult—in the midst of the patriarchal culture of their time—to admit, much less explain, the countercultural behavior of Jesus.[17]

53

There seems to be no doubt that Jesus did what Jewish males, especially religious teachers, were not expected to do.[18] He openly admitted women to the circle of his followers, not just to the larger group that came to hear him in the early portion of his ministry, but to the more intimate group to whom he related in personal friendship and to whom he communicated in greater detail the new law. No Jewish teacher of his day would have counted women among his disciples; for the religious teacher's role was one of expounding the implications of the law, and women were excluded on principle from engaging in this activity. Jesus, on the contrary, is described (in Luke's account, 10:38-42) as visiting the two sisters, Martha and Mary, and communicating his message of salvation to the latter.

One can argue that the similar passage in the Gospel of John brings us into contact with the outlook of the Johannine community, just as does the scene of Jesus and the Samaritan woman, but not necessarily with that of Jesus himself. It is true that the Johannine Gospel is a dramatized theological reflection on what occurred in Jesus' life, death, and resurrection; but it is hardly believable that an element of the narrative as important as Jesus' dealings with the Samaritan woman would have been introduced if it had not been grounded in Jesus' own behavior toward women.[19] What strengthens the historicity of the accounts of Jesus' dealings with women is the admission of the disciples' puzzlement about his conversation with the Samaritan woman; Jesus' male followers were obviously uneasy about his socially deviant attitude toward women.

Besides, one is not limited to the Johannine tradition in tracing Jesus' "new" approach to women. Redaction criticism of the Lukan corpus points up the prominence of women in that account. The Lukan account of the Last Supper, for example, may well point to early Christian recollection of women's presence at that key event as well as at the crucifixion of Jesus.[20]

Even if, as some feminist scholars have suggested, the attitude of Luke to women is ambiguous, perhaps in places a bit negative,[21] the Gospel points to the fact that the role of women was one that

54

the early Christian communities had to contend with precisely because of what they inherited from Jesus himself and from the historical happenings connected with Jesus' death and resurrection. Behind the radical egalitarianism of Gal. 3:26 lies Jesus' own acceptance of women as equal human beings.

If, then, Jesus did not absorb the sense of male superiority intrinsic to his Jewish/Galilean culture, the question arises, What would explain this? Apparently there were no natural forces at work apart from the bond of love between himself and his mother (a bond, however, which would have been interpreted for any young Jewish male according to the law) or apart from the egalitarianism intrinsic to the friendships he had with women. Even the respect and love between his parents to which he was exposed as he grew up would normally have been expressed by them and experienced by him within the cultural patterns of Galilean Judaism. True, there are passages in the Bible that suggest an antipatriarchal strain in the tradition;[22] but Jesus' acquaintance with such texts would scarcely explain the fundamental discrepancy between his views and his cultural context.

Theological reflection at this point turns toward the impact of Jesus' Abba experience. Like the charismatic experience of prophetism, the Abba experience would have challenged the socioreligious world view of Jewish culture and its patriarchal rooting. If Jewish patriarchy was grounded most ultimately in the assumption of Yahweh's nature and role as superpatriarch, and if Jesus experienced the transcendent God as other than that, culturally derived discriminations about women could not have survived in Jesus' consciousness. Jesus apparently did not think of his Abba as loving women less than men, and it was precisely this divine friendship offered distinctively to each human person that was (and is) the deepest source of human equality, independent of ethnic origin or socio-economic status or gender. The very transcendence of the God whom Jesus experienced as Abba denied any attachment or implication of gender preference to the divine. Yet it was in his own experienced "neutrality" toward women and men that Jesus understood his Abba's egalitarian love for humans.

As we will see more fully in a later chapter, his own human compassion and care for people functioned as sacramental word to him about the will of his Father.

Sexuality We have scarcely begun to probe the attitude of Jesus toward human sexuality, more precisely toward his own relating as a sexual being to the men and women who entered his life. For the moment, we are partially blocked in such reflection by the broader inadequacy of our overall understandings of human sexual relationships. Theoretically we can glimpse, through texts such as Ephesians 5, the transformation injected into human sexuality by the self-giving and therefore life-giving death of Jesus. We are, however, a long way from grasping the manner in which the divine self-giving involved in the Abba experience functioned in the dying Jesus' sexuality-transforming response to his Abba's love.

Still, recent theological reflection has advanced far enough to suggest that Jesus' world view, and especially his understanding of God, were incompatible with the assumptions of patriarchal culture. The New Testament literature, even though it is already influenced by Christianity's movement away from its profoundly revolutionary beginnings, leaves no doubt about the radical social implications of Jesus' antipatriarchal stance. The most obvious and symbolic dimension of patriarchy is the relation that exists between women and men, and the various forms of women's subordination that reinforce the dominant position of men. However, recent studies have clarified the inseparability of discrimination against women from the overall social and economic oppressions linked *Power* with class, race, and poverty.[23] Intrinsic to that negation of people is a given culture's understanding of power. As important a challenge to patriarchy as Jesus' behavior toward women was, the challenge went beyond that. What was at stake was the interpretation of authority and power as motor and glue of society. Authority and power must be—this the gospel outlook admits, but not the kind of dominative rule characteristic of human history up to this *Authority* point—"the Son of Man has come not to be served but to serve and to give his life for the redemption of many" (Matt. 29:28). One cannot legitimately use human law, as it has existed for centuries *attitude towards the Poor*

in the context of patriarchal assumptions, as a mirror of the divine will and then turn around and ground, actually legitimate, human law (including what is assumed to be "natural law") in "divine law." Jesus' Abba experience exposes this abuse of religious belief as social legitimation.

Being a radical challenge to the image of God as superpatriarch, Jesus' awareness of his Abba sensitized him to the injustice of discrimination in all its forms. There is no doubt that this was the case: recent study of the Gospels has highlighted the importance of Jesus' "preferential option for the poor," his constant and deliberate association with the marginated of his day. When criticized by some of the official religious leadership for eating and drinking with sinners, Jesus responded with parables like those collected in Luke 15.[24] One of the parables that most tellingly expresses Jesus' rejection of social stereotyping and stratification is the story of the Good Samaritan in which a man, supposedly inferior, is judged superior in his behavior to representatives of the Jewish religious elite.

Jesus' attitude toward the poor involved more than sympathy or even recognition of them as equal human beings; what it involved was an attack upon the source of their second-rate status. The source of patriarchal superiority from which they suffered was the acceptance, by both powerful and powerless, of dominating power as the key to social order and human achievement. To use today's terminology, that was the ruling ideology which maintained the existent social stratification. Jesus' revolutionary opposition to this ideology came not in violence but in refusing such power as the key to his own mission and, instead, achieving that mission by living out the ideal of the Suffering Servant.

Sacramentalizing and embodying divine word and divine compassion, Jesus revealed the paradoxical power of servanthood to create life. That is the way his Abba acts in human history. That is the way of "ruling" that is proper to the kingdom of God. That is the understanding of "the kingdom of God" conveyed by Jesus' own career as "God's parable."[25]

Jesus: the sacrament of divine compassion
Jesus: God's parable

57

A quick review of some pivotal New Testament texts demonstrates this radical revision of societal power. (1) The scene of Jesus' temptation in the desert, which introduces the dynamics of his public life and the power struggle that will lead to his death. Here the suggestion of the Tempter is that Jesus' mission as Messiah will be best fulfilled by the use of economic and political power, "all the kingdoms of the earth." Interestingly, the Gospel of Matthew, of the four Gospels the most reflective of the emergent official structures of infant Christianity, situates this offer of earthly power as the climax of the temptation scene (contrary to the order found in Luke). This reliance on the power of wealth and domination is rejected by Jesus as the approach to his mission and as the interpretation of messianic fulfillment. (2) This point of view is reiterated as Jesus undertakes, in the second half of his public career, to reinterpret for his disciples the meaning of "Messiah" as this applied to himself. As already mentioned, a key instance of this is the scene narrated in Matt. 20:28, where in response to his disciples disputation among themselves as to their relative power positions in the anticipated kingdom, Jesus tells them that in his kingdom those in leadership positions should exercise servanthood (with reference to Isaiah 52-53). (3) This enigmatic understanding of power was obviously understood by earliest Christianity, since the famous "kenotic" passage of Philippians 2 roots the risen Christ's power as Lord in his "service unto death." (4) And if, in examining such texts, one retains the notion that Jesus exists and acts as the embodiment of the divine word of self-revelation, it follows that the divine creative power itself functions in a way diametrically opposed to domination.

Feminist scholars have recently added to such analysis in a number of important ways, to some extent because of distinctive elements in female experience.[26] Three instances may illustrate this. (1) In her essay, "Living Metaphors, Life-giving Symbols," Phyllis Kaminiski argues persuasively the point that women's experience of giving birth opens up a new avenue for developing a *theologia crucis*, one which throws new light on Jesus' saying, "I am in anguish until it be accomplished." Just as human birth brings new life into the world, so Jesus' dying results in the emergence of a new dimension of human life, the life of "resurrection."[27] (2) A number of scholars have drawn attention to the way in which Jesus' "disregard" for the legal taboo of menstruation is a repudiation of women's supposed uncleanness and consequent exclusion from the realm of the ritually sacred. This bears directly on the whole question of societal power, because possession of and control over "the sacred" is probably the most ultimate claim to dominative power. (3) Jesus' attitude toward man/woman roles and responsibility in marriage, studied in the context of his culture, points to an equality of the two partners that stands in opposition to the domination/subordination intrinsic to patriarchal structures of familial power.

In brief, Jesus reveals the paradoxical power of servanthood to create life and personhood, and the hidden power of domination to destroy and kill. The divine way of exercising power is by creative self-gift, the divine way of ruling is by servanthood rather than lordship. This is the wisdom central to the gospel of the kingdom.

Jesus (sacrament of God)

· reveals power of servanthood

to create life + power of domination to destroy

Jesus regarded himself as a (charismatic) prophet in the line of Israel's great prophets

① In what form did this category of self-definition take for Jesus?

② What impact would this have on his religious experience?

4

JESUS' EXPERIENCE AS ISRAELITE PROPHET

Jesus' experience was not simply one of being a Galilean Jew in first-century Palestine and of sharing in the religious faith and life of his day as a Jewish male. Within that context he also had the distinctive experience of being a charismatic prophet. In fact, despite widespread wariness about trying to reach Jesus' self-awareness, there is rather broad agreement today among New Testament scholars that Jesus regarded himself as a prophet in the line of Israel's great prophets.[1] However, this generic consensus requires further specification; there is need to describe more precisely the form that this category of self-definition took for Jesus and then to probe the impact this would have had on his religious experience.

Public Recognition of His Prophetic Role

Matthew and Mark pay little explicit attention to the prophetic identity of Jesus; neither applies the term to Jesus except by way of reporting others' reactions to Jesus. Yet in both Gospels it is clear, almost taken for granted, that the people who witnessed Jesus' ministry looked upon him as a prophet.[2] In the Matthean text that describes Jesus' questioning of his disciples at Caesarea Philippi regarding the people's reaction to his preaching, all the reported responses concern prophetic identity: "Some say John the Baptist, others Elijah, others Jeremiah, or one of the prophets." Given the fact that the Gospel's author is intent in this pericope to move on

Matt

the people saw J. as prophet

61 *Who do you say I am?*

to Simon Peter's acknowledgment of Jesus as Messiah, there seem good grounds for seeing the identification of Jesus as prophet as taken over from Mark rather than due to Matthean redaction. Also in Mark, the redactional interest lies in contrasting the judgment of the people with the judgment of the disciples. So the report of Jesus being seen as prophetic seems derived from recollection of the actual happenings of his career.[3]

Again, in Matthew's account of the entry into Jerusalem on Palm Sunday, Jesus is identified by the crowds as "the prophet from Nazareth." As in the Petrine text, the theological redaction of the passage seems rather to concentrate on Jesus' Davidic connections and, through the mediation of allusions to the liturgy of Tabernacles, to typological parallels with Israel's return from Babylonian exile. The application to Jesus of the title "prophet" is incidental to the redactional purpose of the passage and reflect, rather, the historical fact that this was a designation actually given by the Galilean pilgrims who were attracted to Jesus, a designation preserved in a local tradition upon which Matthew drew.[4]

Somewhat indirectly but still significantly, the scene of Jesus' trial before the Sanhedrin reflects the pervading popular opinion that Jesus was a prophet. Some of his judges struck him and said, "Now, Messiah, *if you are a prophet*, tell us who hit you." This challenge may well be related to the description of Jesus' "cleansing of the Temple" a few days earlier, in justification of which he indirectly but unmistakably referred to his prophetic credentials.

Though even more sparing than Matthew in attributing "prophet" to Jesus, Mark's Gospel also reflects the people's view that Jesus was a prophet. Like Matt. 14:13, Mark 8:28 reports that Jesus' disciples, in response to the question "Who do people say I am?" answer, "one of the prophets." So there seems little doubt that the common public perception of Jesus was that of "the prophet from Galilee."

Contrary to the incidental reference to Jesus as prophet in Mark and Matthew, Luke/Acts uses "prophet" as a key notion to theologize about the identity and mission of Jesus and of early *role of Spirit*

Christianity. This is done in conjunction with Luke's focus on the role of the Spirit in Christianity's origin.[5]

From the moment of his conception, Jesus was animated and directed by the Spirit of prophecy. Not only is Jesus compared with Moses (as he is also by the other synoptics), but the Lukan infancy narrative links his mission to that of Samuel. Jesus' Galilean mission is described against the backdrop of Isa. 61:1, as is also the scene of Jesus responding to the disciples of John who have come to ask if he is indeed "the expected one." And the Emmaus pericope summarizes the career of Jesus as "a prophet, great in word and deed."

Apart from the explicit description of Jesus as prophet, another feature of the composition of the Gospels deserves attention. While there may not be evidence to support Oscar Cullman's[6] contention that prior to the traditions that feed more immediately into the canonical Gospels there was a stratum of tradition in which "prophet" was the dominant title applied to Jesus, the notion of "prophet" remains the controlling model according to which the other titles drawn from Jewish tradition—especially that of Messiah—are reinterpreted when applied to Jesus.

Perhaps the most illuminating instance of this implicit modeling is contained in the sixth chapter of John, the so-called eucharistic discourse of Jesus after the multiplication of the loaves. The gist of Jesus' discourse on the "word of life" is clearly that he is the very *word* proclaimed by the prophets, the word creative of unending life. Moving very rapidly, almost cryptically, from the sign of manna given through Moses to Jesus himself as sign, the historical argument of the passage is dependent on two suppressed middles: (1) the teaching of Elijah that the God of the manna was also the God who gave the rain and therefore the daily bread, and (2) the passage in Isaiah 55 which moves beyond God's support of life through the rain to the deeper sustaining of life by the word proclaimed through the prophets. The Johannine passage is dependent for its full understanding on familiarity with the theology of God's word as it was developed by Israel's prophetic and priestly traditions.

[handwritten top margin: earliest theologizing @ Jesus was based on assumption he was prophet, on his prophetic behavior]

[handwritten left margin: Conclusion]

The assumption in early Christianity seems to have been, then, that Jesus was obviously a prophet, the eschatological prophet sent from God, and it was *as prophet* that he fulfilled the expectations (prophecies) of Israelitic history. What this would seem to argue is that the recollection of Jesus which acted as a source and a criterion for the earliest theologizing about him was the recollection of his prophetic behavior. *[handwritten: Look at his prophetic behavior]*

[handwritten left margin: WORD not VISION]

A notable feature of the early Christian recollection of Jesus as prophet is the skimpy reference to visionary experiences. Apart from the scenes of baptism and transfiguration—both of them highly theologized, even mythic—Jesus is never described as "seeing" his Abba or referring to any such visual experience. Instead, the aspect of sensation referred to (and even that in a figurative sense) is *hearing;* the theology of God's *word* seems dominant throughout, for Jesus and for early Christian reflection. Here, too, there is not a question of extraordinary occasions of God's word being addressed to him; rather, it is the basic sequence of his daily human experiences interpreted by his Jewish religious understandings and lived with the focusing awareness of his Abba's presence to him that function as "word." The latter portion of his public career seems to have been marked by an increasing dissonance between this personal awareness of his Abba and official religion's words about the God of Israel. As with so many of Israel's charismatic prophets, "religion" became questionable for Jesus as a true voice for faith.

[handwritten left margin: ordinary context / conflict w? official religion]

Jesus' Prophetic Activity

[handwritten: teaching / healing]

In their summary of Jesus' activity during the period of his public mission, the Gospels speak of his teaching and healing. Obviously, this describes him as a teacher and charismatic wonder-worker; but both these roles are cast in prophetic terms. His teaching is not that of the prevalent scribal interpretation of Torah, but he teaches "with authority." He proclaims the will of God on the basis of his own immediate knowledge. And his healings are compared with those of Israel's great early prophets, Elijah and Elisha. There is no

Abba's presence to Jesus as WORD is not in visions
not in extraordinary
but in daily ordinary
context

JESUS' EXPERIENCE AS ISRAELITE PROPHET

possibility of ascertaining the actual details of these healing actions of Jesus, but there appears to be substantial evidence that they were worked as signs, *semeia*, parables in action, to bespeak the presence of God's healing action and the arrival of "the day of the Lord."

One can extend the prophetic character of Jesus' teaching by adverting to the intertwining of prophetic and wisdom thought that began centuries before Jesus and found expression in biblical texts with which he was acquainted. Wisdom, of course, forms a distinct theme in the Gospel accounts, but in key passages such as Matthew 11, it is impossible to disengage it from the prophetic aspects of the happening. The prophetic nature of Jesus' wisdom utterances is reinforced by the remark that his manner of teaching was not like that of the scribes.

Indeed, whether it can be traced back to Jesus himself or only to the early Christian awareness of his prophetic mission, Jesus is described using a number of the literary forms of classical Israelitic prophecy.[7] For instance, the "judgment" or "woe" speeches (for example, Matt. 11:20-24) are reminiscent of the language used by Jeremiah and Ezekiel as well as by their predecessors, Amos and Isaiah. Westermann argues that such speech forms are borrowed from legal circles and that the more basic prophetic form is that of "the messenger." Here, too, the New Testament is replete with statements by Jesus that he has been *sent* to proclaim and (as we will see) to achieve the arrival of "the kingdom." Still, another possible link with established prophetic forms comes with Jesus' "disputation speeches," but with an important difference.[8]

Jesus uses the prophetic genre of disputation speech to teach his hearers and correct their poor grasp of God's demands. The really original element in the antithesis comes at the beginning of the refutations. So often in the Old Testament disputation speeches the refutations began with the messenger formula, "thus says the Lord." In Jesus' disputation speeches the formula is always, "But I say to you." Jesus, with the supreme authority vested in him by the Father, announces his challenge to the Law with the authority of God himself. The formula "But I say to you" looks back critically to what the people hold, and opens the way for the words which come from God. The formula sums up the aim of the prophetic disputation speech, to convert the minds and hearts of the people . . . The genre was used in the Old Testament in times of crisis. With the prophet Jesus it is a genre of the *kairos*, the crisis of the irruption of God's kingdom into the world.[9]

Another element of Jesus' public preaching, his predictions, is clearly in the mode of prophetic utterance.[10] There may be need to examine a particular prediction of Jesus to judge whether one is dealing with a statement of Jesus himself or a text emerging in the early church as a "prooftext," a *vaticinium ex eventu*; or, if the statement originates with Jesus, whether it is truly a prophetic "pre-vision" or simply a shrewd human assessment of the situation. At the same time, the statements and signs (for example, the sterile fig tree) are so numerous that it is difficult to deny that Jesus, at least at times, did make some such predictions.

Even in the distinctive use of parables which characterizes his public teaching, Jesus reflects the literary traditions of his prophetic forerunners in Israel. Several prophets, Ezekiel in particular, use fantastic imagery in an attempt to point to the ineffable sphere of the divine, and in so doing, leave their auditors in a state of perplexity and questioning. Parables as used by Jesus have this same psychological impact; their use of paradox intrigues the auditor but also leaves that person uncertain as to the precise meaning of the parable—indeed, there is no meaning in the ordinary sense of that term, for the parable is an invitation to conversion, to true *metanoia*, a change of mentality.[11]

However, both the preaching and the activity of Jesus as described in the Gospels point to more than prophetic identity; they point to his role as Israel's *eschatological* prophet. This goes beyond predicting the imminent arrival of the final stage—John had already done that.[12] Jesus states unequivocally that this final stage has actually begun with his own ministry. His public activity is the kingdom of God at work, fulfilling the destiny of Israel—even though in the latter stage of his career, in the wake of the crowd's abandonment and the increasing opposition of religious leaders, he is forced to rethink the nature of Israel's salvation and his own role as the Suffering Servant.

Synoptic paralleling of Jesus to Moses, particularly in the Matthean Gospel, unmistakably views him as an eschatological prophetic figure. Even though these Matthean texts reflect the "conversation" going on at that time between the Jewish Christian communities and Jamnian Judaism after the destruction of the Temple, they are rooted in the time and career of Jesus. Moses was looked upon by Jesus' contemporaries as the greatest of prophets, as the paradigm instance of Yahweh's communication with Israel, so that any identification of Jesus as "prophet" would inevitably have entailed comparison with Moses. Obviously, this view focused on the gift of Torah through the agency of Moses; which means that the entire question of early Christianity's posture toward the law was a matter of the prophetic credentials of Jesus in relationship to Moses. To claim for Jesus a position superior to that of Moses, to claim for him the power to initiate a new and more final law—"but *I* say to you"[13]—was equivalent to claiming the role of Israel's final and consummate prophet.[14]

In Jesus' day, even with the Pharisees' transfer of cultic purity to everyday Jewish life, it was still the faithful performance of the Levitical prescriptions for the Temple that formed the heart of observance of the Mosaic Law. Thus we recognize the importance of Sanders's contention that Jesus' prediction of the Temple's destruction is the clearest instance of Jesus' actual reference to himself as the prophet initiating the final epoch.[15] Standing in the Temple court, he not only condemned the violation of the Temple by the buyers and sellers, but he asserted his own authority over the sacred precincts and did so in the name of his Father, clearly conducting himself in a fashion reminiscent of prophets like Jeremiah. The fact that this event was most likely what triggered the wrath of the Temple authorities to the point of plotting his death indicates that these authorities grasped the fundamental challenge that Jesus was making to Judaism's official religious establishment and institutions.

Other indications of Jesus' prophetic identity are the two visionary experiences of the baptism and transfiguration.[16] Granted the mythic/midrashic elements in the scenes as described in the

Gospels, behind the traditions underlying these pericopes lie some actual happenings that provide the hinge events in the Gospel narratives. However one wishes to interpret these scenes—and we will have to deal with them more explicitly in a bit—they unquestionably depict Jesus in a prophetic mode. As a matter of fact, the connection of the baptism scene with the precursor role of John and the linkage of the transfiguration happening with Moses and Elijah cast Jesus in an eschatological light and his career as the arrival of "the day of the Lord."

Without denying the distinctiveness of Jesus' awareness of God and the breakthrough character of his Abba experience, it is highly significant that Jesus, like the great Israelitic prophets before him, taught *within* the parameters of Israelitic tradition.[17] Rather than repudiate the revelation that had come through Moses and prophets, Jesus claims insight into the true and deepest dimensions of the divine word already communicated to the chosen people. "I have not come to destroy the law but to fulfill it" (Matt. 5:17). While this, in its textual derivation, reflects Matthew's preoccupation with relating Jesus to the law, it also sums up the realization-through-transcendence that marked Jesus' relationship to the traditions that he reinterpreted so drastically that his reading of them demanded an intellectual conversion on the part of his Jewish contemporaries. Just such a demand for conversion to the true interpretation of "the word of the Lord" had always been at the heart of the prophetic message; and Jesus, in being radically innovative, was simultaneously profoundly traditional.

In his treatment of Jesus' "visions," Gils makes the important point that a central element, perhaps the most central, in the visionary charisms of the great prophets was their insight into the Israelite traditions that eventually flow into the Hebrew Bible. Applied to Jesus, it is clear that the New Testament texts claim for him an understanding of the biblical texts that surpasses that of the trained scribes, an insight that comes from his prophetic endowment rather than from any technical training.[18] Moreover, this prophetic insight permitted Jesus to find "the word of God" in ordinary human experience of the created world.[19]

Jesus' Symbolic Speech and Activity *espec Parables*

Nothing leads one further into another person's inner consciousness than that person's use of symbol, whether it be metaphorical language or some nonverbal symbol. It is precisely in the effort to communicate those elements of awareness which defy discursive description that we employ symbolic language and actions. For this reason the parables of Jesus, essentially metaphorical in their narrative form, provide a privileged insight into his awareness of the God who is the principal referent of the parables. Like the Israelite prophets before him who image God as father (Jer. 3:19) or mother (Isa. 66:13) or husband (Hosea 2) or shepherd (Ezekiel 34) or potter (Jer. 18:16) or midwife (Isa. 1:2), Jesus' parables of the kingdom portray his Abba in various roles.[20]

A parable which unquestionably bears examination in this regard is that of the wicked vinedressers. Common to all three synoptics, it bears signs of having already been theologized by Mark if not by the tradition from which he draws. While Mark does not emphasize, as does Matthew, the judgment upon Jewish leadership, he already christologizes Jesus' own parable. He draws attention to Jesus' identity as "the specially beloved (and by implication *only*) son," and suggests Jesus' crucifixion outside Jerusalem by the detail that the son was cast outside the vineyard. Mark presents the parable as an allegory of Israelite prophetism, whose history of rejection by the people reaches its final stage in the rejection of Jesus himself. Probably in its original form in Jesus' teaching, the parable stood as a metaphor of the enduring patience of God—Jesus' point in the parable was not his own identity but the character of his Abba.[21] Even in this original form, however, the parable reflected Jesus' awareness of his own culminating prophetic mission.

Linked to such prophetic use of metaphor were symbolic actions like the multiplication of the loaves, the entry into Jerusalem on the Sunday before his death, and the "cleansing" of the Temple.[22] We have already seen the implications that flowed from the symbolism of Jesus' "cleansing" of the Temple. What is important to the present step in our argument is to determine the deliberateness of Jesus' challenge to the establishment, that is, the deliberateness of his claim to Messiahship. This requires studying the scene in conjunction with the preceding account of Jesus' entry into Jerusalem on Palm Sunday, for the two events are inseparable in the narrative tradition.[23]

As the Gospels describe Jesus' preparation for entry into the city (go find the donkey, etc.), it is clear that Jesus had finally decided to lay public claim to his messianic role and to do so through the symbolism of riding on "the royal animal," reminiscent of Solomon's claim to the throne and of the prophecy of Zechariah to which the Gospel texts refer. That the symbolism was grasped by those who observed him is confirmed by the actions of the pilgrim crowd as they accompanied him and acclaimed his Davidic identity. The messianic symbolism of the occasion was not, then, accidental; it was deliberately intended and planned by Jesus, and therefore reflects his consciousness of being the fulfillment, though in prophetic form, of Israel's expectations of a coming Davidic savior. This was joined to, indeed coalesced with, the awareness of being "a prophet like unto Moses," which lay at the root of his "But I say to you."

Having entered the city, Jesus proceeded to the Temple (that day or the next) and drove from the Temple courts the buyers and sellers who were making the sacred precincts a market where the poor and innocent were fleeced by unscrupulous money-changers and merchants. Jesus' action was, however, more than an impassioned ethical reaction against abuse; it was a challenge to the entire social structure of Temple ceremony, and it was seen as such by the Temple officialdom. The question of the high priests to Jesus was "By what authority . . . ?" His response, though couched in the form of a question in response to their question, is quite clear: his authority was that of a prophet whose way had been prepared by John's prophetic proclamation of the advent of one who would establish the kingdom. Jesus' answer to the Temple leadership flowed from his awareness of being the one who bears this eschatological authority.

Jesus' Self-awareness as Eschatological Prophet

We have, then, moved already and inevitably into a study of Jesus' *awareness* of being prophetic.[24] This is admittedly a perilous endeavor, doomed to partial success at best. To achieve anything like accurate completeness is beyond the realm of possibility; but one can assume in Jesus' case, as in that of other humans, that his actions and speech reflect substantially his consciousness at any given moment. So our task is one of examining sayings or actions that, at least in their substance, can be traced back to Jesus himself and that therefore give us evidence for the outlook and aims that governed him in his public life.[25]

One of the earliest indications of Jesus' awareness of himself as prophet comes in relationship to John the Baptist. Whether or not one wishes to maintain that Jesus began as a disciple of John, it seems quite clear that he saw his own activity as continuing and fulfilling what John had initiated.[26] This is confirmed by the fact that John's own disciples were attracted to him in the first instance, or they came on mission from John to ask Jesus if indeed he was the one expected. Since there is no doubt that John's activity was interpreted in a prophetic light by the general public, by the Jewish authorities, and by Jesus himself, this would indicate that Jesus saw himself and his ministry as prophetic.

Second, if the crowds who heard Jesus teach were aware that his manner of teaching was not that typical of the rabbis of his day, Jesus himself must surely have been conscious of this. The sayings attributed to him in the Gospels clearly point to this: on any number of occasions he dissociated himself from the more complicated exegetical interpretations of the scribes. In the light of what we have already studied about Jesus' Abba experience, one can argue that the source of his distinctive teaching was his immediate exposure to the divine; but for the moment we simply wish to stress that the teaching of Jesus indicates that he was in contact with the

71

religious realities about which he spoke and felt confident in saying, "Thus says the Lord God," that is, this is the will of my Father. The "messenger" form of speech, which we recognized as perhaps most basic to prophetic utterance, takes on with Jesus a new force because of his claim to immediate insight into the divine. It seems difficult to deny that behind Jesus' behavior as a prophet was his awareness of being a prophet.

Third, Jesus was conscious of being moved by divine power. In the next chapter we will have occasion to study in greater detail the relation of Jesus to God's Spirit. For now it will suffice to remember that for centuries Israelite tradition had linked the Spirit of God with the vocation and ministry of the prophets. The very notion of "inspired scriptures" seems rooted in this connection. Drawing from this element of religious understanding that he would have gained from reflection on the prophetic writings, if from no other source, Jesus would have understood in a prophetic sense his own experience of being moved by the Father's power working in him.

Fourth, the question arises: Did Jesus himself understand the features of his public ministry as fulfillment of Isaiah 61? A surface reading of Luke's Gospel (Luke 4:16-30) would lead immediately to an affirmative response. Here Jesus is described, at the very beginning of his public career, as using this text in the synagogue of Nazareth to announce the character of his intended activity. However, careful analysis of this Lukan passage indicates that the use of the text is part of Luke's redactional activity, as it is in Acts 10:38 and in the account of John the Baptist's disciples visiting Jesus.[27] Still, if the Lukan tradition was able to make this connection, is it too much to imagine that Jesus himself, conversant as he was with the biblical texts, would never have seen how his healing the sick, speaking for the oppressed, preaching the gospel to the poor, were in effect giving meaning to this Isaian prediction of the eschatological prophet? This argument is strengthened textually by the paralleling of Luke 7:18-35 (John's disciples coming to Jesus) with Matthew 11, indicating that the origin of this scene is not Luke's own redactional perspective, though it is compatible with that. Rather, we are driven back to Q and to the likelihood that Jesus did actually appeal to his actions in response to John's query; and that Luke, in fleshing out the Nazareth scene, was drawing from this more original though oblique reference to Isaiah 61.[28]

Fifth, still another debatable element of Jesus' self-awareness has to do with his identity as the Servant described in Isaiah 52-53. As late as the 1960s there was still fairly wide agreement that Jesus probably thought of himself in these terms, and that passages like Matt. 20:28 witnessed to that self-identification. More recently, exegetes have been reluctant to trace this designation back to Jesus himself, though most agree that it is found in the earliest identifiable strata of tradition, which would explain its prominence in all four of the Gospels.[30]

The reluctance to attribute this interpretation of his career to Jesus himself is not easy to understand. Vincent Taylor's remark in 1937 still rings true: the process of reinterpreting "Messiah" in terms of the Isaian Servant must have been the work of some religious genius; and why attribute this insight to some unknown genius of the first Christian decade rather than to the person (Jesus) to whom the earliest traditions attribute it?[31] Besides, at the same time that they deny "Suffering Servant" to Jesus' own self-identification, many contemporary scholars contend that he thought of himself in terms of "the suffering righteous one."[32] There seems to be a very thin line between the "suffering righteous one" (linked perhaps with sect memories of "the teacher of righteousness") and the Suffering Righteous Servant of Isaiah 52. If the early Christian community used the Isaian passage to puzzle out the enigma of Jesus' death, why would not Jesus himself have used it to puzzle out the official rejection and hostility that were clearly leading to his own fate? If Matthew used the parallel with Jeremiah to interpret Jesus' passion, is there any good reason why Jesus himself might not have resonated with the Jeremiah-like fate of the Isaian Servant? Perhaps there is need to remember that the process of theologically interpreting Jesus began with Jesus himself.

Another element in the Gospel texts that points to Jesus' awareness of being the eschatological prophet is the use of "kingdom of

God" in his parables. Adopting Perrin's interpretation—namely, that the term is used as a tensive symbol pointing to Yahweh's ongoing saving activity in the history of Israel—Jesus in his parabolic teaching is describing for his hearers the action of God in "the day of the Lord" which is already upon them. The kingdom is not just something to be anticipated as imminent; it is already "in your midst" because it has broken through in Jesus' own ministry. The messianic age has begun, the eschatological period of Israel's history is in progress, and Jesus is the agent of its realization.[33]

If this was Jesus' self-awareness, it may be possible to gain additional insight into the much-debated issue of Jesus' identification of himself as "Son of Man." For some time, there has been a widespread tendency to distinguish between the Son of Man in history, with which Jesus identifies, and another "heavenly" or eschatological figure of a "Son of Man." Yet if one takes seriously Jesus' identification of himself, in his trial before the Sanhedrin, as the Son of Man coming on the clouds of heaven, this distinction between two "Sons of Man" does not seem to have textual justification. On balance, the position of Jack Kingsbury in his writings on the synoptics seems capable of taking account of the relevant texts as well as the insights of a range of exegetes. In brief, he points out that "Son of Man" is not used as a predicate title to identify Jesus; instead, the subject who is Jesus uses this title to refer to himself without it being a "confessional" claim to a role or a dignity. On the other hand, "Son of Man" is not simply a substitute in Jesus' speech for "I"; it is a public title, involves a claim to divine authority, and in some instances points to his eschatological vindication.[34]

It is solidly possible that Jesus, aware of his role as eschatological prophet, realized that in some fashion he embodied the destiny of his people. As such he was a concrete personification of his people rather than the fictive personification of faithful Jews which is the figure of the "Son of Man" in Daniel 7.[35] The empowered Son of Man is not something beyond history; rather, the Son of Man has *exousia* on earth to overcome evil (Mark 2:10)—the kingdom of heaven is already operative in the ministry of Jesus.

Finally, in addition to the symbolic actions already mentioned, there is the multiplication of the loaves which plays such a central role in all four Gospels. We have long since learned the impossibility of reconstructing a chronology of Jesus' public ministry. Yet there is a very minimal sequence of happenings found in all of the evangelists, and in all four this skeletal sequence contains a hinge series about midway through the narrative. Jesus is followed by the crowds into what is called "a desert place," and their hunger is provided for in some unusual way. Given this "sign," they mistakenly seek to make Jesus "king," which he refuses. As a result, the crowds abandon him. He asks his disciples how the people do regard him, and Peter responds with the first acknowledgment of Jesus as Messiah. Shortly thereafter the transfiguration occurs in the midst of Jesus' predictions of his coming passion, and Peter remonstrates with Jesus for such views and is sharply rebuked. Given this pattern, which in somewhat different fashion runs through the synoptics and John, it is solidly probable that something unusual occurred in the multiplication of the bread, even if we are unable to ascertain its exact character. It is also probable that Jesus intended the action as a sign that related his own mission to that of Moses, as a symbol that he fulfilled the expectation of "a prophet like Moses." This inner awareness found expression in the discourse in the Capernaum synagogue which underlies the early portion of John 6, the awareness of prophetic mission surpassing even that of Moses.

Theological Reflection

Given this textual-historical evidence about Jesus' awareness of being Israel's eschatological prophet, how can theological reflection probe further the consciousness Jesus had of the transcendent reality he addressed as Abba? For the most part, this would seem to consist in situating the career of Jesus, and therefore the human awareness that accompanied that career, within its religio-cultural context.

Traditional Israelite Prophecy

The impression of Jesus' auditors that he was a prophet, and his own awareness of being eschatological prophet, occurred within the limits of Jewish understanding and memory. As a result, examination of the experience of Israel's great charismatic prophets should cast some light on the prophetic experience of Jesus. Textual sources allow us to deal with two situations of Old Testament prophets' experience: (1) the occasion of their "call," and (2) the pattern of their prophetic career. So we study theologically, with concentration on Jeremiah and Ezekiel, the vocation experience of Israel's charismatic prophets and their experience of actually prophesying. This may help us understand better what "being prophet" might have meant for Jesus.

1. *Awareness of the divine.* Characteristic of the vocation experience was its unexpectedness, yet its "fit" with the prophet's previous faith.[36] The God who calls is recognized as the God who called Moses and earlier prophets, and through them the people Israel. This is the Yahweh of Israelite tradition, the Lord of the law, the God of Abraham and Isaac and Jacob and David; yet a God still unrecognized by Israel for what God truly is. Particularly with Ezekiel and Isaiah, the prophet's imagination produced symbolic visual imagery of the divine. In the tradition of Hosea, Jeremiah, and Deutero Isaiah, there apparently was some experience of hearing words. Reflection on the passages in these prophetic writings, however, indicates that there was a deeper dimension to the experience of divine presence that transcended imagery, thought, and language—in fact, an intrusion into the prophet's psyche that triggered image and memory. The prophet was aware of God-present, God unavoidably occupying the prophet's consciousness, God immediately and "personally" communicating the divine will.[37]

This adds a new dimension to the prophets' understanding of their people's religious traditions, for these traditions speak about the God whom they, the prophets, *know.*[38] It gives a new perspective to the prophets' awareness of the happenings of their own day, for they had been admitted to the circle of God's "counselors"; they are privy to the divine decisions about the course of history not because they foresee these, but because they know the God who is the Lord and how that God acts.[39]

Not only in their vocation experience, but also in their consequent activity, it is this same-yet-different awareness of Yahweh by which the prophets measure the people's fidelity to the covenant, the accuracy and genuinity of the direction given by the official leadership, the wisdom of political judgments, and the appropriateness of Israel's institutions. Most basically, the prophet's acquaintance with Israel's God stands always at the basis of prophetic proclamation to a people who do not understand this God in the same way and to a leadership that distorts the reality of Yahweh for its own purposes. The experience of the prophets that animates their awareness and activity from their vocation onward is the inescapable presence of God.

2. *Sense of being missioned to speak.* Intrinsic to the prophetic vocation is the sense of being sent to proclaim the will of Yahweh to a people not too eager to hear this word. More than one prophet, beginning with Moses, expressed reluctance, even inability, to carry out this prophetic impulse; but the vocation is insistent. The hand of God (the Spirit) is upon the prophet; there is no negating it. Even at the risk of death, as with Jeremiah, the prophet is victim of the compulsion to transmit the word of God.

Throughout the career of the prophet, the sense remains of being the legate of Yahweh. For the most part, then, the prophet does not speak in his own name but in the name of God. The classic literary form of prophetic speech is that of the oracle, the proclamation of God's messenger. The message is not basically new, for it is a call to return to observance of the covenant. Yet it is a message renewed in the context of an ever new historical situation. The will of God is unchanging, but its precise demands need constant interpretation in the light of events. It is the prophet above all who is called to discern "the signs of the times," but to do so according to the counsel and wisdom of Yahweh. Inevitably, the prophet's preaching comes into conflict with those who for one reason or another interpret these signs differently. Jeremiah is the classic case of the prophet's counsel; it favored alliance with Babylon, clashing with the determination of Jerusalem's leaders to throw in their lot with Egypt.[40]

3. Instrument of "judgment" and "restoration." The voice of the prophet in Israel is always one that calls to conversion. For that very reason, the prophetic message deals with God's future activity. Often it is a message that the "day of the Lord" will be a dreaded day of retribution, of punishment for Israel's sins. One form of "judgment speech" that has particular relevance for study of the New Testament is the use of parable as, for example, in Isaiah 5, where the narrative metaphor is clearly a reference to the behavior and deserved punishment of Israel. At the same time, this is accompanied by the promise that restoration will follow upon Israel's repentance and conversion. At the moment of the prophets' call and continuing throughout their career is the implication that Israel is in need of being "restored" to its pristine faith and trust in Yahweh, that Israel's institutions need once more to serve their original purpose—in spite of the fact that such fidelity had never particularly marked the people's history.

This element of restoration is most marked in the two great prophets of the exile, Ezekiel and Deutero Isaiah. Once the city of Jerusalem had fallen in 587, the oracles of Ezekiel, which up to that time had threatened unrepentant Judah with destruction, turned to proclamation of comfort and of hope for the future restoration of Jerusalem and its Temple. So, too, the "Book of Consolation" that occupies chapters 40-55 in the Book of Isaiah promises the imminent reclaiming and rebuilding of Jerusalem by the Babylonian exiles. Given the creative power of the word of God which, as Isaiah 55 says, "does not return to God without accomplishing that for which it was sent," the promise of restoration given through Ezekiel and Deutero Isaiah is more than prediction, even more than promise. It is already the power to accomplish that restoration unleashed in history. The prophet is aware of the power of this word which is uttered; it has the power to build or destroy, to plant or to uproot. The prophet is himself or herself the agent within the community for Israel's restoration.

Jesus as Israelite Prophet

While he could not have used the technical approaches of modern biblical scholarship to identify the various elements in the experience of Israel's charismatic prophets, there is much of what we have just seen that Jesus—if he was himself charismatic eschatological prophet—would have intuited in reflecting on the prophetic traditions in the Hebrew Bible. Moreover, the same basic patterns of the experience of Israel's prophets would have found realization in his own vocation and ministry.

Before returning to the scene of the baptism to study it as an event of prophetic vocation, what we have earlier seen and will continue to see about the basic and continuous awareness of his Abba radically changes consideration of any *one* happening in Jesus' public life as his "call." The call had always been there in the presence of Abba. While for him, as for all humans, each new experience was to some extent unexpected, there is reflected in the Gospel description of Jesus as prophet none of the unanticipated that sometimes marked the initial vocation and later episodes in the career of Israel's prophets. At the same time, there is no question but that the baptism at the Jordan is described in the Gospels as a prophetic call initiating Jesus' public ministry.

The Markan account already sets the scene in a prophetic frame of reference.[41] The opening words that introduce John the Baptist carry the reader back to Isa. 40:3 and the prophecy of restoration that opens the "Book of Consolation." Enter, then, the figure of the prophet John who is preaching repentance because of the imminent arrival of the kingdom. His prophetic mission is characterized as preparing for and giving way to the fuller mission of Jesus.

There is little question about the actual historical occurrence of Jesus' baptism by John, even though the passage as we have it in the Gospels is highly theologized. Textual study indicates that the texts as they occur in the New Testament are traceable to the earliest stage of tradition. However, the factuality of the observable baptizing of Jesus does not provide us with any solid ground for accepting the passage as a report of Jesus' own awareness.[42]

79

Luke's account, however, points to the experiential dimension of the baptism (to Jesus' inner awareness) in a way the other accounts do not, for he links the theophany to Jesus' "prayer" rather than to the baptizing itself. It is in his contemplative union with his Abba that Jesus is aware of being God's Son, God's beloved one—aware of possessing God's Spirit in a unique way. This does not in any way run counter to the clearly prophetic tone of the other accounts. For Luke, the Spirit is the Spirit of prophecy and the two themes of Spirit and prophet are inseparable in his theology. What the Lukan Gospel suggests is that the theological interpretation of the baptism scene that linked Jesus with the history of Israel's prophets characterized Jesus' own awareness long before it shaped the post-resurrection traditions. Simply put, Jesus himself was conscious of being chosen by his Abba for the prophetic mission of announcing and effecting the arrival of the kingdom of God.

Leaving as an open question the extent to which details of Luke's account provide an insight into Jesus' experience at the baptism, there is little doubt but that the event is depicted in the Gospel passages as one of prophetic "calling."[43] Not only is there the broader link with Israelite prophetism, but the synoptic texts, beginning with Mark, are linked to Isa. 42:1 and therefore to the idealized prophetic figure of the Suffering Servant—perhaps also to Gen. 22:2 which would introduce the Isaac typology.[44]

Even if Luke's description of the baptismal scene and consequent theophany is to be ascribed to his redactional theology, there is no question that it fits into his overall theme of Jesus' *prophetic* ministry. For Luke, it is the Spirit who draws Jesus to the Jordan, who leads to the testing in the desert, and who then leads him to Nazareth; there, in the synagogue, Jesus makes his claim to fulfill the prophetic role described in Isaiah 61. While this passage is too indicative of Luke's theological creativity to be used as evidence of Jesus' awareness, Jesus' consciousness that his ministry paralleled the activity mentioned in Isaiah 61 plus his familiarity with the prophetic writings make it difficult to believe that he would not himself have made the connection.

However one wishes to deal with the synoptic reference to Jesus' sonship in the baptismal scene, it is difficult to deny that the three elements we identified as characteristic of the vocation of Israel's charismatic prophets are verified in this initiation of Jesus' public ministry. Clearly, Jesus' awareness of the divine was immediate and intimate, beyond anything granted his predecessors. There seems no doubt that he had a sense of being sent. The rest of the gospel narrative is an account of his response to that summons, and his preaching that the kingdom of God was at hand was a proclamation that God was at work not just to restore Israel to previous glory but to accomplish on earth the triumph granted the heavenly personification of the people, the Son of Man in Daniel 7.

The prophetic elements of the baptism scene find reiteration and strengthening in the account of the transfiguration. There Jesus is depicted as the realization of what was foreshadowed in Moses and Elijah, the law and the prophets. The theophany is again of Abba and the Spirit (this time in the manifestation of the cloud, the *kabod* Yahweh). Jesus' teaching receives divine approbation, "Hear him," and the scene marks the beginning of Jesus' journey to Jerusalem where he was sent to undertake the mysterious restoration of Israel through the paradox of death as the Servant. Though it is disputed whether the title "Servant" can be traced to Jesus himself, from this point onward Jesus works to help his disciples understand that his Messiahship is to be interpreted in terms of the figure of the Servant of Isaiah 52-53. What lends credibility to Jesus' actual attribution of "Servant" to himself is the narrative's account of how completely alien and puzzling this notion was to the disciples' understanding prior to the resurrection experience.

One final Gospel scene may help establish the fact of Jesus' own self-identification as "echatological prophet" and provide some insight into what this meant for him. The scene is that of his trial before the Sanhedrin. The exact details of Jesus' trial are notoriously difficult to establish,[45] and some recent efforts to determine them have been encumbered by ideologically loaded attempts to accuse or exonerate various parties in the proceedings. Still, it is difficult to deny that there was some kind of trial before Jewish religious leaders, that this probably dealt most centrally with his prophetic activity vis-à-vis the Temple, and that accusers and accused were dealing with Jesus' claims to be the eschatological restorer of Israel—the prophetic and messianic Son of Man.[46] As described in the synoptic narrative, Jesus, challenged as to his prophetic authority, replies not as he had earlier in the cure of the paralytic by claiming to exercise on earth the *exousia* granted the Son of Man in Dan. 7:14, but by predicting his eschatological glory as the Son of Man.

Finally, that Jesus felt himself to be about the business of restoring Israel, and this within a prophetic context, seems undeniable. The fundamental dynamic of altering the interpretation of Messiah from kingly-political to religious-prophetic, which was central to Jesus' formation of his disciples, points to Jesus' awareness that he was implementing an unanticipated divine strategy of restoration. There are indications that Jesus himself had to adjust his own understanding of his prophetic mission as he, like Jeremiah and others before, experienced rejection by the religious leadership of his day. Faced with this rejection, he increasingly moved toward identification with the Servant of Deutero Isaiah 52-53. But if the passages in question do reflect Jesus' own understanding, they also indicate that what was involved was a deepened insight into the intrinsic role of suffering in the prophetic vocation.

Jesus' Symbolic Activity

If Jesus' use of parables is understood as an attempt to communicate the prophetic insight he had into the reality of the divine, his consciously symbolic activity is an equally telling indication of his awareness of being the eschatological prophet. Doing things that were patently linked in their symbolism with prophetic aspects of Israelite tradition was not accidental. Jesus deliberately performed actions like the cleansing of the Temple, or the multiplication of the loaves, or sharing table fellowship with the marginated of society. Such actions, precisely because their main purpose was to convey meaning, provide a privileged reflection of the mental state of Jesus which was their source.

Three such instances may illustrate the point. All three have received detailed exegetical study in recent years, and there is general agreement on the interpretation of each of the three. Without repeating detailed textual explanation for (1) Jesus' choice of the Twelve, (2) his prediction of the Temple destruction, and (3) his sharing meals with "sinners," these three actions of Jesus can be examined from the point of view of their symbolic character.

1. Without falling back into the anachronistic argument that Jesus set up an institutionalized church by selecting twelve special disciples as the "first bishops," one can assert with high probability that he did single out a group of *twelve*.[47] Not only do scholars accept the historical reality of such an inner circle selected by Jesus, but they agree that on at least one occasion he sent them on an apostolic extension of his own mission.[48] There can be little doubt that the number of these close disciples was intended as a reference to the twelve tribes and as pointing to fulfillment in some form or other of the destiny of the chosen people. The notion that such a group "would sit on thrones judging the twelve tribes of Israel" (Luke 22:30) was of its very nature eschatological and reflected Jesus' awareness of being the agent of eschatological realization.[49] Moreover, the selection of such a group to carry on the ministry exercised by Jesus himself allows us to conclude that Jesus did not have an apocalyptic expectation of an imminent end to human history, but cherished instead the conviction that his Abba was sending him to initiate the final stage of the kingdom. What was happening through him and then through the Twelve was the restoration of Israel and the fulfillment of all in Israel's history that was prophetic, that is, that was promise. The precise time for the full realization of his Abba's intent was not the issue, nor was it an element in Jesus' awareness. What he was conscious of was the unleashing in history of the power of God's Spirit.

2. Both Meyer and Sanders have argued convincingly for the historical factuality and highly symbolic character of Jesus' prediction of the destruction of the Jerusalem Temple. They see it as the

event that triggered the decision to kill Jesus, which means that the Temple leadership grasped the symbolic import of Jesus' action. Driving out the money-changers from the Temple courts was clearly a singular affair. Jesus must have known that the exploitative commerce connected with pilgrimages to the Temple would resume immediately and the Gospel texts indicate that he made no attempt to make his "cleansing" action permanent. It was meant to be a symbolic act, an acted-out parable intended to arouse the very response in the Temple leadership that it did, and to set the stage for the explicit threat to the Temple's existence.

What the prediction of the Temple's overthrow involved was nothing less than reversal of the then prevalent official eschatology, an eschatology that since the return from exile had focused on restoration of the second Temple. Jesus' prophetic proclamation pointed instead to a new and unofficial fulfillment by God of the promises made through the great charismatic prophets of Israel. Whatever that fulfillment was to be, Jesus was aware that it was already occurring in his own Spirit-directed mission, a mission that existed in opposition to the activity and ideology of the Temple priesthood.

3. For a variety of reasons, not least the scholarly effort to examine the biblical base for Christian celebration of Eucharist, the past two decades have seen increased interest in Jesus' "table fellowship." In ways not yet fleshed out by research and reflection, the pattern of Jesus' sharing meals with sinners fits into a millennia-long use of "eating," and especially of "bread," as symbols for the divine saving activity—manna in the desert, Jesus' multiplication of the loaves and his consequent discourse on the "bread of life," the Last Supper and centuries of commemorating it (along with Jesus' passage through death into risen life) in the Christian Eucharist. What is being emphasized today, and what fits naturally into our present investigation, is the way in which Jesus' association with the marginated of society was a lived-out parable of God's special care for "that which was lost"—for the powerless and dispossessed of human society who, because they are less socially influential, are generally considered less important and tend to be

neglected, if not exploited, even by religious leadership. Isaiah 61 denotes the way in which prophetic thought had seen divine care for the poor as a sign of "the day of the Lord," and Luke's extensive reference to this text seems to be linked with his redactional grouping (in chapter 15) of parables about "that which was lost."

If one agrees that Jesus' table fellowship had a parabolic dimension, something that seems to be confirmed by the parables in Luke 15 which respond to the Pharisees' criticism of Jesus for associating with these "lower levels" of society, then we are dealing with a metaphor used by Jesus to convey his awareness of the God he knew as Abba—a God whose ways are not humans' ways (Isaiah 55). This opens up the topic of our next chapter, namely, the way in which Jesus' own attitudes and experience acted as sacramental word that revealed to him the reality of God.

To summarize: As Israel's eschatological prophet, Jesus was constantly aware of the inescapable and absorbing presence of Israel's God, his Abba. He was conscious of being "sent" by the guiding and empowering Spirit of his Father to proclaim the creative prophetic word. He felt compelled to pass prophetic judgment, above all on false images of his Abba. He understood, if only in as yet unspecified generality, that his was the task of initiating the longed-for restoration of his people, and to do so by prophetic activity. He spoke and acted metaphorically (parabolically) in an attempt to share the awareness he had of God as unconditioned lover.

5

JESUS' SPIRIT-EMPOWERED MINISTRY

The second chapter of Paul's letter to the Philippians contains the famous kenotic passage which is now widely accepted as traceable to a primitive Christian liturgical hymn, perhaps from the Jerusalem community. In it, the attitude of the human Jesus in accepting his Servant role even unto death is described as "obedience"; and the text indicates that this "obedience" was expressed most tellingly and salvifically in the experience of suffering and death.[1]

We are not dealing here with Jesus' own characterization of his approach to life and death, but with very early Christian interpretation and with a poetic expression of that interpretation. Still, one cannot help but ask whether this earliest *theologia crucis* was influenced by what the disciples had experienced of Jesus' own understanding of his behavior. It is clear that this primitive Christian understanding was present in the earliest decades of the communities' existence. Already the theme of Jesus' obedience as the basis of his redemptive activity, especially through his death, is central to Paul's soteriology, finding expression particularly in Romans 5-6.[2] Perhaps under Pauline influence, the Epistle to the Hebrews focuses on Jesus' internal attitude, more specifically his obedience, as the essence of his high priestly sacrificial act. "Here in chapter 10, however, where the discussion may be said to have reached its climax, the significance of Jesus' death is located unambiguously in the *obedience* of his offering."[3] This chapter in Hebrews makes explicit what Philippians 2 only suggests, namely, that obedience was something that Jesus *learned* through human experience, particularly the experience of his death.

In the Jewish usage of the term in Jesus' day, "obedience" to God would have been inseparable from observance of the law and therefore inseparable from the socio-cultural context of Jesus' experience.[4] What seems to be involved in the notion of Jesus' obedience is his *faith*, his unqualified acceptance of the transcendent being *for* him as Abba. Also involved is his unqualified response to the divine invitation in the praxis of his daily activity and, of course, in the pattern of decisions that underlay this activity. To put it in today's terminology, his fundamental moral option was a yes to his Abba's will.

As with any human being, Jesus' perception of reality and its demands was a constantly unfolding process; each moment's exposure to the world around him was conditioned by all of his previous perceptions and responses. This meant that his response to the "demanding" presence of his Abba and the self-perception that was intrinsic to that Abba experience was an evolving attitude; very literally Jesus was *becoming "son"* throughout his life. In any human situation, being son or daughter of a given set of parents is much more than a matter of simple biological origin; on the personal level, it is a matter of accepted and lived out personal relationships. Many a parent has not acknowledged a child; many a son or daughter has refused, in the practical order, to accept the parent given by procreation. Such acceptance of parentage involves the deepest levels of psychological response, for it is inseparable from one's own self-identification. Such was Jesus' "obedience" as the New Testament literature reflects it, a continuing positive response to each happening as given by his Abba, an acknowledgment of Abba's being his loving Father.

Even though Jesus' awareness of God was not that of legislator or judge—even the prophetic strains of Israelitic thought had long before moved the God/Israel covenant relationship into a more personal rather than purely legal context—the Father/son relation intrinsic to Abba was an all-encompassing law. Response to a lover, if it is totally faithful, requires a regard for and positive resonance with the desires of that lover. Such a response is neither negatively demeaning nor self-denying, for one trusts that the lover desires what is best for oneself as the beloved. That such trust in Abba existed in Jesus' obedience seems beyond question when one probes the dynamics of Jesus' prayer in Gethsemane. For Jesus, love of Abba and his obedience to Abba coincided completely. Not to do what he perceived to be his Father's will was unimaginable.

The general tenor of the Gospel narratives reflects such an unconditioned yes to his Abba's will on Jesus' part. Of the scenes that express this explicitly, one might single out—in addition to the decisive passage of Gethsemane—the instruction given his disciples just before and after Peter's confession and the transfiguration, instruction in which Jesus begins to lead them to a reinterpretation of messiah in terms of the Suffering Servant.

For the moment, we will refrain from deciding whether or not references to Jesus as the Servant are traceable to his own statements to the disciples. Nevertheless, it seems clear that midway in his public career Jesus began to challenge the disciples' mistaken application of "messiah" to his mission and to point them instead toward his impending passion and death. Given this, it is difficult to avoid the argument of Joachim Jeremias that Jesus, thoroughly familiar as he was with the prophetic writings, would not have made the connection with Isaiah 52-53.[5]

If it is true that as his public life advanced Jesus became increasingly aware that much of the Jewish leadership was set against his teaching and upset enough to eliminate him, by death if necessary, then this must have required a radical reevaluation on his part of the manner in which the establishment of the kingdom was to take place. Like the prophet Jeremiah before him—Jeremiah, whose career may have provided the exemplar for the Servant Songs[6]— Jesus faced the need to question not just the manner in which the religious institutions of Judaism were being conducted but the intrinsic validity of those institutions. Whether one is to understand the text's use of the Greek *dei* to refer to the fact that it was God's will that salvation should come by way of Jesus' death or whether the word suggests the intrinsic link of death-undertaken-through-love with the destruction of evil, Jesus apparently became convinced that his death was an unavoidable price that he had to pay if he was to carry out the eschatological mission given him by his Abba.

That all this was humanly repellent to Jesus is textually reflected in his response to Peter when that disciple "reprimanded" Jesus for saying that he must go down to Jerusalem to be put to death. The seemingly harsh response, "Get behind me, Satan," places Peter's words in the context of temptation, ultimately the same temptation of Satan in the desert when the Tempter proposed means of fulfilling Jesus' messianic task other than those "planned" by his Father. Like the desert Satan, Peter suggested the incompatibility of suffering and death with strategy appropriate to the Messiah. Jesus himself was not immune to the attraction of an alternative—Gethsemane makes this clear—but realized, if only unclearly, that some intrinsic link bound the arrival of the kingdom with his own suffering and death. The reality of the human condition, with human enslavement to sin rendering people incapable by themselves of overcoming the forces of evil, demanded that Jesus allow the Spirit, the power of divine love, to confront and destroy evil in his own death. Perhaps without explicitly understanding this—how could he, prior to his resurrection?—Jesus permitted himself to be drawn to Jerusalem by his Abba's Spirit.

One seems to be justified, then, in stating that Jesus' human consciousness was marked by unwavering acceptance of the demands of reality as he experienced it. Believing as a Jew of his time that God, his Abba, was the ruler of history and of daily events, nothing that happened was seen as apart from "the will of God," therefore requiring an obedient response. Such a view of overarching and omnipresent divine providence is clearly reflected in statements from the Sermon on the Mount—"not a sparrow falls," "the lilies of the field, see how they are attired," and the like.

That the text of the sermon as we have it in the synoptic Gospels is a literary creation of the traditions from which the evangelists drew is undeniable. At the same time, it would be hard to deny that it was Jesus' own teaching, his imagery, his view of human life, and his awareness of his Abba that grounded the community memory which found expression in these early Christian traditions. For Jesus, "divine providence" was not a theological doctrine or even a faith symbol; quite simply, it was his Abba's caring presence, a presence that pervaded and was translated by and experienced in his own care for people.

Possessed by the Spirit

Another avenue for exploring this aspect of Jesus' awareness is to examine his relationship to "the Spirit." It is difficult for many of us in such an investigation to bracket any understandings of "the Holy Spirit" as a *divine person* that we may have gained from classical trinitarian theology. Jesus' awareness was that of being moved by the power of his Abba, of possessing this power and being able to direct it toward caring for people, but also of being possessed by this power as were Israel's great charismatic prophets.[7] It was also, as far as we can gather, the experience of sharing and implementing his Abba's creatively outgoing love.

Like any other element of Jesus' experience, his awareness of God's Spirit occurred within the context of contemporaneous Jewish awareness of God's Spirit being active in their midst. Broader and more general than this was the basic religious sense of God's "dwelling with them" which, at least to some extent, found a focus in the Jerusalem Temple. Yet some (nonbiblical) texts indicate that opinion was divided regarding the Spirit's presence with the people; in some circles there was concern about the apparent absence of the Spirit, at least of the more observable charismatic manifestations of this Spirit.

The biblical background of Jewish thinking about God's Spirit was uneven.[8] There seems to have been considerable interest in the charismatic manifestations of the Spirit in the earliest period of Israelite prophetism, perhaps even earlier in the period of the judges; this focused on the seizures that marked the activity of special figures like the *nebiim*. From the eighth century B.C.E. until

At time of Jesus: 3 manifestations of God's Spirit
① constant presence of God w. Creation & chosen people
② intervention seen mostly in charismatic prophet

GOD'S BELOVED

③ impulse toward attitudes & behavior that constituted true WISDOM

the time of the Babylonian exile, the biblical writings relatively infrequently mention the Spirit. With Ezekiel and with the priestly tradition and its account of creation, one again encounters explicit and frequent mention of Yahweh's "spirit," understood now more broadly. It is still the Spirit that animates the prophet and impels the charismatic individual to prophetic proclamation, but it is also God's continuing creative and life-giving power, able to bring the universe into existence and sustain it and to restore Israel to life after the death of exile.

A third element enters the picture with the wisdom literature: the intertwining of "spirit" with "wisdom." The two are not identical, but God's Spirit working within humans teaches them true wisdom; above all, it is the Spirit that inclines people toward those moral attitudes that constitute the heart of wisdom. In a sense, wisdom, though itself "spirit," is more external and finds expression above all in the law. Spirit, on the other hand, is the inner law that impels people to follow the law and its guidance toward wisdom. Yet, Spirit and wisdom remain very closely linked; "they would be identical were it not for the fact that wisdom does not have what the Spirit has, namely, the character of a force or inner energy, the power to transform."[9]

Thus at the time of Jesus, believing Jews thought of three somewhat distinct manifestations of God's Spirit: there was the constant abiding presence of God with creation and in a special way with his chosen people; there was the intervention of God's Spirit that occurred most noticeably in the vocation and career of charismatic figures like the prophets; and there was the impulse toward attitudes and behavior that constituted true wisdom. These three converged and came to bear on the hope of God's achieving the restoration of Israel, a hope shared by Jesus and linked with his understanding of "the kingdom of God."

Something of the prevalent Jewish cultural understanding of "spirit" can be glimpsed in the writings of Paul, though obviously the term has been radically changed for him by the experience of the risen Christ. Despite the newness of Paul's insight into the "spiriting" of the human Jesus that came with passage into risen

92

life, this insight built upon and drew from the understanding of "spirit" that Paul already possessed. The classic difficulty of deciding exactly what *pneuma* refers to in a number of Pauline texts indicates the fluidity of the notion and the overlap between "God's Spirit" and "God as Spirit," as well as the overlap between "spirit" as a constitutive element of the human existent and "Spirit" as involved in the risen Christ's sharing with humans the divine power/principle that in him has overcome death. One cannot justifiably read these Pauline views into the historical experience of Jesus, but they do help flesh out our understanding of the religio-cultural world view within which Jesus was aware of possessing and being possessed by God's spirit.

In the New Testament literature it is the Gospel of John that leads reflective Christian faith into the most extensive and profound contact with the Spirit of his Father, which was Jesus' own Spirit and which was the principle of their oneness. Recent study has detailed the pneumatology of the Fourth Gospel and provided some insight into the awareness that Jesus might have had of his endowment and possession by his Father's Spirit.[10] Yet in working from John's Gospel we are admittedly a half century away from the initiating experience and thus in a position to do little more than argue back to an experience of Jesus that more probably underlies the Johannine texts.

Though it is itself clearly a theological presentation of the Spirit, Luke/Acts may bring us a bit closer to Jesus' own awareness—or at least a step closer to what we can judge was probably Jesus' awareness. One immediately encounters the problem that reference to the Spirit's role in the Lukan account is very obviously a basic element in the redactional activity of the author, connected—as we saw in an earlier chapter—with Luke's emphasis on the prophetic mission of Jesus and the early church. However, this very link may lead us to a justifiable insight: if possession of and by the Spirit of God was thought of as intrinsic to the charism of Israelitic prophecy, and if Jesus did identify himself in terms of Israel's prophetic tradition, he would consequently have been aware of the Spirit's presence in his own life's experience.[11]

Moreover, one needs to ask the source of Luke's description of the Spirit as pervasive in the life and ministry of Jesus. Did it come from early Christian memory of Jesus' reference to the Spirit or from Q or from some source distinctive to Luke? Or did it come as a result of the charismatic experience of the early Christians themselves, an experience of receiving the Spirit from the risen Christ; and the connection—so central to Paul's theology—of resurrection with Spirit-life and new creation?

Even granted the theological character of Luke's account of the Spirit, there are a number of elements in his Gospel that are common to the synoptic traditions and that may carry us back to Jesus himself. One of the clearest of these is the conflict between Jesus and his opponents regarding the source of his healing power. When accused of working wonders through evil spirits, Jesus not only repudiated the charge but accused his opponents of sinning against the Holy Spirit.

Luke's account is especially valuable for the insight it gives into the two aspects of Jesus' empowerment, represented by the two Greek words *exousia* and *dynamis*. Though distinguishable as terms, representing the distinction between the two realities they denominate, *exousia* and *dynamis* in their biblical usage are inseparable; their corresponding realities interpenetrate in the divine exercise of power in human history.[12] While *exousia* names the kind of power associated with official authority, *dynamis* points rather to physical power. But given the biblical theology of God's creative word that works through the prophets, and the description in the Gospels of Jesus healing by the power of his words, it seems that the New Testament perspective is that there was one power, the power of God's Spirit, that worked through Jesus' teaching and healing.

Like the Israelitic prophets, Jesus had apparently a constant sense of being "on the inside track" with regard to the divine intent in history's guidance. Not only was he aware, at least in a general way, of the direction of the kingdom of God, but he was also aware of embodying the divine intent in his own activity. The New Testament texts do not reflect an awareness on Jesus' part (as was the case with a prophet like Micah) of being part of God's "privy council."[13] The few references to "the angels" do not treat them as a consultant body for divine decision, though there is a passing indication of angelic awareness of divine "strategy" when Jesus mentions that neither he nor the angels have knowledge of the time of history's termination (Matt. 24:36). Rather, the texts seem to indicate that Jesus sensed that no one, human or angelic, shared his own immediate intimacy with Abba. Only Jesus is "in the bosom of the Father" (John 1:18).

One feature of Jesus' experience of being moved by his Abba's spirit was his sense of existing for others. Beneath any particular formulation of this in the Gospel texts lies the attitude experienced by those around him. His care for people, especially for those most in need, drove him beyond what his disciples judged good for his health. Yet his response to their remonstrances was that the people were like sheep without a shepherd (Matt. 9:37). As eschatological prophet, his destiny and the purpose of his human existence was inseparable from that of his people. As the Son of Man embodiment of that people, he clearly existed for their sake with *exousia* to witness to the truth and with *dynamis* to heal their wounds. As Servant, his life was meant to be a giving of self, even to death, through which salvation would come to others. Even if the explicit application to Jesus of these titles came only with the theological reflection of first-generation Christianity, this reflection grew out of Jesus' disciples' recollection of his words and deeds.[14]

If, as seems to have been the case, Jesus' sense of existing for others was intrinsic to his awareness of living out his Abba's will and being moved by his Abba's Spirit, an important conclusion can be drawn regarding the character of his religious experience. It means that Jesus' awareness of the transcendent as his Abba came as a dimension of his ongoing daily dealings with people, and in terms of such relationships. Above all, it was in experiencing his own deep concern for people, empathizing with their human needs and frailties, longing for their happiness and fulfillment, that he understood the mind of his Father whose Spirit he shared. In other words, the primary model for thinking about the divine—that which challenged the models provided by his religion and culture—was his own human self-awareness. It was this self-awareness as he gave of self to others that embodied in its most basic expression the divine word of self-giving, the new and definitive revelation about what it means for God to be for humans, and even what it means for God to be God.

To express it in more technical theological terminology: for Jesus himself—and derivatively for those who subsequently accepted him as "the gospel"—his praxis was the sacrament that revealed and made present the true God. The rooting of that praxis in Jesus' completely faithful and non-self-centered love for others meant that creative power was seen to reside in love and in self-gift rather than in domination. Moreover, what Jesus experienced was that this transforming divine love found its historical location and point of contact with people's lives precisely in humans' love for one another. It was the heart of Jesus' mission as embodied word of God to proclaim this; and only the experience of such love going to death and becoming thereby the source of risen life could reveal the power of love to shatter evil and death, and to create fully personal, that is, Spirited life.

As Christian faith has understood it from the beginning, it was in the experience of his Passover through death into resurrection that Jesus became fully the Christ, the human instrument of humans' salvation. It was in this triumph of love over death that he became the "human for all other humans," that his very risen existence consisted in sharing his life-creating Spirit with others, that his human risen "bodiliness" lay in his communion with those women and men who accept relationship with him in faith. We can only wonder what the religious experience of the risen Christ is, but theologically we can argue that his awareness of God as Abba, though certainly in a different dimension than it was during the days of his life and ministry in Palestine, is as inseparable from his conscious self-giving to others as it ever was. Truly, as Paul remarked centuries ago, humans fill up the mystery of Christ.

All of this is acceptable as theological speculation, but are there any solid grounds for all of this in the evidences provided by the *evidence is in the Parables*

New Testament literature? Probably the firmest basis for saying yes comes from Jesus' parables.[15] Again and again, Jesus appeals to human models of justice, compassion, and the like as images reflecting the kingdom of God—the king who absolves the debt, the man who gives the banquet, the planter of the vineyard, the prodigal's father, the shepherd seeking the lost sheep. However, as we examine these, it is clear that Jesus' use of such human attitudes to portray the mind of his Abba flows from his own experience of having such attitudes.

Another, more technical way of expressing this is to say that Jesus' entire life and ministry was a sacrament of divine compassion. This is brought out in detail in Monika Hellwig's volume *Jesus the Compassion of God*. However, one can go a step further, showing that this sacramentality is highlighted in the parables that speak metaphorically about this compassionate God; and still further by pointing out that the deepest aspect of this sacramentality consists in the way in which, for Jesus himself, the compassion he feels for the afflicted specifies his awareness of his Abba's healing power working through him.

In a sense, Jesus is constantly saying, "If I think and feel that way, certainly my Father does also." Perhaps this comes through most clearly in the sequence of parables contained in Luke 15. Commentators are generally agreed that Jesus told these parables about "that which was lost and then found" as a response to the charge that he was associating with "sinners and tax-collectors."[16] His answer to these accusations, whose implication was that he could not truly be from God, was to describe God as acting in the very way he himself acted. While the first two metaphors, the shepherd seeking out the lost sheep and the women searching for the lost coin, make the message unmistakable, it is the third parable, that of the father of the prodigal son, that most sharply and tellingly conveys the image of a God who does not operate according to the pattern of laws, customs, and sanctions devised by humans. Instead, God acts as does Jesus himself—indeed, acts sacramentally in Jesus' activity.

Placing Jesus' religious experience in this daily down-to-earth context does much to rehabilitate ordinary human experience. It also raises certain basic questions about the normative function of Jesus' experience. Christian tradition is firm that the definitive revelation of the divine took place in Jesus and that the gospel of what God has accomplished in Jesus as the Christ is the criterion of all later theological and doctrinal explanations of that gospel. However, if one denies to Jesus' own human understanding the prerogatives of "eternal, infinite, universal knowledge"—which centuries of mythic theologizing did attribute to it—and recognizes its historical relativity and limitation, one must probe more deeply than we have so far to determine the exact relationships between Christian origins and later religious understandings. If the experience of God did take place for Jesus within the context of his Jewish world view—and where else could it have taken place?—and precisely in terms of the human experiences of Jesus in that particular time and place, it follows that Jesus' exposure to the divine found in his consciousness only one cultural translation. So we must be careful to distinguish those elements of cultural translation from the unique, underlying awareness of God of which they were an inadequate expression. The latter (the underlying awareness of God) is perennially normative for Christian faith; the former (the cultural translations of that awareness) are to be learned from, recognizing that they did have some ability to communicate the deeper experience. We must also be aware that they bear both the insights and the distorting inadequacies of any human culture and therefore need to be critically appraised rather than slavishly repeated.

Encounter with Evil

Quite a different aspect of Jesus' religious experience confronts us when we turn to his reaction to the evil he encountered. Though this reaction was as diverse as the various forms of evil he met— whether these were the more "excusable" sins of people that were linked to their fears, undisciplined desires, and social pressures or the more informed and deliberate malice, exploitation, and dishonesty of the rich and powerful—a basic aversion to evil in any form seems to have been characteristic of Jesus' consciousness. The notion of a cosmic battle between the God of Israel and the forces of evil was carried over from the Jewish literature, biblical and intertestamental, into the theology of the New Testament writings and was most probably a structuring element in Jesus' own inter-pretation of life's experience. Since his prophetic task was to initiate the definitive stage of God's kingdom, that is, God's rule over all creation, a confrontation with the forces that opposed this divine rule was intrinsic to his mission. However, Jesus' response to genuine evil, other than his compassion for human moral weak-nesses, involved more than simple hostility for "the enemy." Evil was an affront to his Abba, an attempt to thwart the divine efforts to bring happiness and love and freedom to humans, and therefore a cause of both pain and anger for Jesus. Precisely because his relation to Abba was so unique and intimate and profound, his sensitivity to evil and his repugnance to it were so keen and disturbing.[17]

Behind the passion of his attacks on those who deliberately refused to hear his message, and especially those teachers of the law whom he accused of hypocrisy and of leading the ordinary people astray, lay Jesus' emotional response to evil. Like the "woe statements" of Israel's prophets, his threats of divine vengeance were directed against those who rejected the Spirit that worked through him, a rejection that involved a refusal of his Abba's saving self-gift.[18]

There was, however, a second side to Jesus' experience of evil: his awareness of special power over it. While the account of Jesus' exorcisms is unquestionably colored by the cultural view of evil spirits current in the Mediterranean world of his day, there seems little doubt that he worked some extraordinary deeds of freeing people from the evils that afflicted them. There is no way to discover exactly when and under what conditions Jesus became aware of his healing power and began to exercise it. All indications from the Gospel texts are that his ministry, which followed immediately upon the baptism by John, was marked from the beginning by miracles, and that prior to that time none of these deeds which manifested his power as a charismatic healer were performed.[19]

If Jesus did on frequent occasions drive out the evil spirits by his command, he must have had a continuing awareness that the power to do this was at his disposal. As we have already seen, his reply to John's disciples—"Go, tell John what you have observed . . ."—relates to the text of Isaiah 61 where the healing power in question is the Spirit of God. This indicates that Jesus' sense of being "inspired" came in his experience of caring response to those he encountered in need of "cure." He was moved, both psychologically and physically (or should these be distinguished?), to effective compassion by the Spirit he shared with his Abba. It was in healing people that he grew increasingly conscious of what salvation from God meant and how the kingdom of God was being established. Through healing, he also became aware of the inevitability of love's triumph over death and sin, and where the ultimate power lay. In this experience, he came to understand what kind of a God his Abba was—transcendent and creatively compassionate. This, of course, is the insight central to a "theology of liberation," for one cannot understand or theologize about a liberating God unless one is engaged in the task of liberation. Another way of stating this is to say that Christian ministry is a sacrament.

Because it is so central to the radical reassessment of social forces taking place in today's world, it might be profitable to probe more deeply Jesus' understanding of and judgment upon *power*. That this was central to Jesus' approach to his mission and ministry is clear from the temptation scene: the Tempter proposes to Jesus that the key to fulfillment of his messianic role lies in the possession of economic and political power, "all the kingdoms of the earth." And as Luke's Gospel expresses it, after the temptation had been rejected, it returned in other forms throughout Jesus' public career—"Satan left him for a time."

The challenge of Jesus' behavior is that his apparently naive faith in the power of truth and love proved to be justified. The wisdom of "this world" gave way in Jesus' triumph over death to the wisdom of "the little ones." In writing to the Corinthians, Paul was fully aware of the paradoxical character of Christ's wisdom—a stumbling block to Jews and foolishness to Greeks, yet the path to life. And before Paul, Jesus himself discovered in his own experience that true and ultimate power is not a matter of domination but of service; his Abba, who was none other than the Lord of creation, exercised servant-power through him as *the* servant.

The greatest service one can render another is the gift of self in love and care, for life comes from this gift for both giver and recipient. Thus in his own unfolding experience of loving his sisters and brothers even unto death, Jesus discovered a God who is the source of the most profound of revolutions—a God who challenges radically all the values and structures that flow from domination and does so in the unfathomable mystery of laying self open to suffering in the death of Jesus, "the dearly beloved one." Even Jesus could have grasped the depths of this revelation only with passage into risen awareness, where from the experience of death chosen in love there has emerged the experience of life previously unimaginable.

This leads us, then, to the continuing mystery of the evolving historical awareness of "the body of Christ," which involves Christ's own continuing awareness of being Savior by being the incarnated Word. Here is where we begin to encounter Christology in the strictest sense . . . which lies beyond the present book.

CONCLUSIONS

What, then, can we conclude about the religious experience of Jesus of Nazareth? Three aspects of this experience need to be distinguished, though they were inseparably linked in their historical reality: Jesus' awareness of the transcendent, that is, God; Jesus' awareness of himself in relation to this transcendent; and Jesus' experience of the religious forms of his Galilean-Jewish culture by which these first two aspects were shaped and in which they were expressed (even though these external elements of Jewish religion proved to be old wine skins for very new wine).

We begin with the third and most ascertainable of these. Jesus was clearly a Galilean Jew, with all that says about the earliest emergence and development of his world view and specifically his understanding of God. The straightforward and relatively unsophisticated acceptance of the biblical traditions about Yahweh's dealings with his chosen people that characterized Galilean faith and belief would certainly have been Jesus' as he grew into adulthood. This would have been shaped by the explicit and implicit instructions about his people and his God that his home provided and by his regular participation in the local synagogue. However, at some point Jesus began to be exposed to the more sophisticated Judaism of Jerusalem both in the teaching of the Pharisaic scribes and in the rituals and explanation of the Torah that took place in the Temple.

This experience of religious practice must itself be distinguished. Persons who sincerely engaged in such activity which celebrated the salvation history of God's people inevitably identified with two things: (1) the deep faith and relatedness to God of *they had this rich living tradition - their CULTURE*

(true believers in previous and their own generations, particularly the faith and belief of religious "heroes" like the prophets; and (2) the institutionalization—the biblical texts, the rituals, the social structures and processes, the official explanations of scripture and ritual and social structures—of faith and belief. Ideally, these two coincide, but at times they can coexist uneasily or even in tension in the one living process of a person's religious awareness. And when the institutional elements are observably inadequate or even counterproductive, the religious experience of a person can be one of confusion, turmoil, rebellion, or profound conversion.

Some of this tension apparently occurred in Jesus' experience of his Jewish religion. As far as we can gather, as he was growing up he accepted without much questioning the inherited belief about Yahweh, the God who had guided his people's history. If one can retroject from the attitudes of his adult years, it seems also that his deepest identification was with the spiritual insight of the great prophets. These apparently coincided basically with his own im- mediate experience of God: the God he knew as Abba was the same God that Jeremiah and Isaiah and Hosea knew. More than that, in his earlier years he apparently had no difficulty identifying with the rituals and the reflection on the Torah that took place in synagogue and Temple. But as his insight into his own experience of God deepened and matured—as his personal exegesis of the biblical texts and insight into his Jewish religious tradition were impacted by this direct experience of God and as his exposure to the actual conduct of Jewish religious leadership broadened—the tension between faith and religious institutions was increasingly felt. This clearly occurred in the conflict, whatever its precise character, between Jesus and powerful elements of Jewish religious officialdom.

tension between faith & religs instit

As for Jesus' religious beliefs, that is, the ideas and images that gave shape to his understanding of the divine, everything seems to indicate that he was and remained up to the end of his life profoundly Jewish. There is nothing in his teaching, at least as it is reflected in the New Testament texts, that cannot be linked with the thinking and imagery of the Mosaic, prophetic, and wisdom

traditions of the Bible. Even in his prayer, Jesus shared with his
coreligionists the formulations of the Psalms and the Benedictions. *diverse*
However, the beliefs of Judaism in Jesus' days were manifold and
not totally consistent; even in its biblical formulation, Israelitic-
Jewish belief was dialectical. Early Mosaic traditions survived but
were challenged by later insights of prophetism; wisdom literature
probed the adequacy of Deuteronomic "justice"; the Psalms at
times reflect a God of gentle care for his errant people and at other
times a God of avenging might. Within this diversity, Jesus seems
to have resonated more with the prophetic strain that runs from
Hosea through Jeremiah, and with the Deuteronomic formulation
of the law with which it probably was linked. In the exegetical
discussions of his day, this would have allied him with the school *thus*
of Hillel rather than with that of Shammai.

Thus from one point of view, Jesus' personal awareness of God *to* *awareness*
and his unrestricted response of commitment to that experienced *of God*
God was limited by his Jewish beliefs and religious practice. Yet
from another point of view, his own awareness and faith
transcended his Jewish religious culture, something that was not
strange to the prophetic elements of that culture. In the case of
Jesus, the New Testament texts indicate that his awareness of
transcendent reality went beyond that of the greatest Israelitic
prophets, that it can be characterized as at least distinctive and *unique*
perhaps even unique. Jesus' mature experience of institutionalized
religion was, then, mixed. The various forms of ritual, doctrine,
prayer, life style, and theocentric social structure that were so basic
to Jewish culture were unquestionably cherished by him and
recognized as fundamentally congruent with his subjective awareness of his Abba. Yet their inability to translate not only his unique
awareness of the divine but also the deepest dimensions of Israelitic tradition seems to have been increasingly felt by him as he
became more aware of the religious attitudes of his contemporaries—particularly of those who were considered to be the
guardians and interpreters of God's word to the people.

At the root of this growing dis-ease with official understanding
and implementation of Jewish religion was Jesus' awareness of

God. While the Gospel texts that tell us about Jesus' experience of the transcendent are not numerous, they nevertheless point with high probability to a knowledge that was immediate, intimate, and personal. Scholars debate whether this awareness of the divine deserves to be called unique or only distinctive; but it clearly was of a nature that separated Jesus' understanding of God from that of his contemporaries.

Perhaps most basic in Jesus' awareness of God was the knowledge that this God loved him in a special way; he was God's beloved one. The God in question was unquestioningly identified with Yahweh, the one God of Israelitic-Jewish tradition. Jesus' application to this God of the word "Abba," however, reflects a drastic revision of the traditional view of Yahweh as a patriarchal sovereign. Yet the influence of Jewish patriarchal culture remained to some extent, because the love relationship in question was interpreted in terms of father/son. Certainly, Jesus' own masculinity, experienced within Galilean Judaism, played a role in the identification of God/lover as Abba; but the reality of the God he knew as Abba also acted in Jesus' consciousness as a profound challenge to the cultural understanding of his maleness that he had inherited. We are only beginning to probe this dynamic with the questions and insights provided by today's feminist scholarship.

The God whom Jesus experienced was a God continuously active in human history, working lovingly and compassionately to bring about his rule, his kingdom, in the lives of women and men. Jesus experienced the saving power, the Spirit, of this God as the source of his own ministry of caring for "the little ones." He experienced his own witness to truth as a key element in the way God's kingdom was being brought to fulfillment. He experienced his Abba as combatting evil in all of its forms and doing so precisely by the Spirit. And he experienced this battle with evil as coming to eschatological climax in his own ministry. More likely, Jesus' awareness of God's saving activity in the world, particularly through him, was more eschatological than apocalyptic; the sense of "fulfillment in the end time" was qualitative rather than chronological.

Clearly, then, Jesus' experience of the transcendent God was profoundly personal. He did not experience something; he experienced *someone*. In the last analysis, this is the ground for Christian theism. It continues and reinforces the theistic experience of Israel it flows into the theistic experience of centuries of Christian prayer. This aspect of transcendent reality lies beyond the insight attainable through philosophical reflection, and for that reason it remains a matter of religious belief—belief in the ultimate mystery that the transcendent freely revealed divine selfhood to humans.

Finally, Jesus' experience of himself in relation to the transcendent was not that of being religious, but of being who he was. Certainly, in all the formal Jewish religious activities in which he engaged he had the experience, as did those around him, of being religiously Jewish. But this was not the final consideration; the most basic element was his self-identification. It was precisely his self-identification that made Jesus' experience of the transcendent God unique. Israel's great prophets, like Isaiah or Jeremiah, had also had an immediate exposure to the reality of God. For them, however, this experience was not fundamentally constitutive of their self-identity; it was an orientation to mission, a sense of special destiny, an awareness of close relationship to God, but it came to them as a modification of a personal identity already essentially established. For Jesus it was different, as far as we can piece together the bits of evidence provided by insight into the consciousness that underlay his public ministry. To be Abba's special one, Abba's son in a way that no one else was, this is what it meant for Jesus to be who he was. Thus his experience of the divine was intrinsic to experiencing himself and therefore a controlling element in all of his religious experience.

Because experience of the divine was so integral to Jesus' self-awareness, which as in any human developed as his life's experience unfolded, his experience of God as Abba was likewise a developing understanding. While the basic identification of the God in question did not shift from one ultimate reality to another, the God who was the pole of his own "sonship" became known more fully as Jesus' self-understanding as son emerged in the course of his life experience. The sequence of experiences that made up his human lifetime revealed ever new dimensions of his own selfhood and demanded choices about the self he was determined to become; and as he understood more deeply what "being son" meant for him and faced the free options involved in responding to that understanding, his awareness of what Abba was for him inevitably grew. If one can extrapolate in the context of faith, it would seem that a full insight into himself as son and, simultaneously, a complete awareness of his Abba came to him only with the passage into risen existence.

This implies, then, that the ongoing human experience of Jesus was sacramental, that is, that the awareness of his Abba's presence to him permeated and gave a distinctive dimension to the meaning of each experience, but in turn was interpreted by each experience. God was known by Jesus as the "person" he experienced as lovingly present at each moment of his life's unfolding. Since part of Jesus' adult self-understanding was that of being the eschatological prophet, the one commissioned by God's own Spirit to be the instrument for the definitive establishment of the kingdom, his sense of mission was intertwined with his awareness of his Abba, and each experience of caring for "the little ones" was a sacrament of Abba's saving compassion.

Finally, despite its immediacy and what we might call its inescapability, Jesus' experience of God as Abba involved something analogous to faith. This comes through especially in the confrontation with his passion and death. There are hints, perhaps more than hints, that he had to deal with the temptation that his experience might be an illusion. It would have been most unusual if some element of this hesitancy had not come to him as he was dying abandoned on the cross, when all the normal human indications suggested that his public ministry had ended in failure. Yet the critical scene of Gethsemane indicates that the awareness of his Abba endured throughout the passion and governed his choice to go to his death, and that Jesus died trusting that God was a faithful lover who would not abandon him in death.

With his death, there begins a stage in the mystery of Jesus' identity and mission for which the basis of understanding is not evidences of his own earthly career; rather, it is the ongoing experience of Christian communities that believe in his continuing presence in their midst and their empowerment by his Spirit. What the "religious experience" of Jesus is in this situation, the experience of being the Christ in risen existence, we can only imagine dimly by extrapolation from our own experience of sharing faith in Christian community and of being moved by his Spirit. However, I believe we can say with the assurance proper to Christian faith that Jesus' awareness now, as in his life on earth, focuses on and is grounded in the loving awareness of his Abba.

Notes to Chapter 1

1. James D. G. Dunn, *Christology in the Making* (Philadelphia, 1980), 22.

2. Robert Jewett, ed., *Christology and Exegesis*, Semeia 30 (Atlanta, 1984).

3. To indicate the broad base of the discussion, I have selected four persons whose principal involvement is with New Testament studies and two who are considered systematic theologians. Of the four exegetes, Joachim Jeremias is from Germany, Jacques Guillet from France, James D. G. Dunn from England, and W. Marchel, a Belgian who did the work in question in Rome under the direction of S. Lyonnet. Of the two systematicians, Edward Schillebeeckx is a leading figure in German/Dutch theological circles and Jan Sobrino is representative of Latin American liberation theology.

Selecting these six is not a judgment on the value of other important studies, such as David Stanley's essay "'Go and Tell John What You Hear and See': Jesus' Self-understanding in the Light of His Earthly History," in *Who Do People Say I Am*, ed. F. Eigo (Villanova, Pa., 1980), 47-90; or Ben Meyer's *The Aims of Jesus* (London, 1979); or Karl Rahner's early studies on Jesus' self-awareness.

4. *Abba. Studien zur neutestamentlichen Theologie und Zeitgeschichte* (Göttingen, 1966) and *Das Vater-Unser im Lichte der neuren Forschung* (Stuttgart, 1962). Key chapters from these two are translated in the volume *The Prayers of Jesus* (Philadelphia, 1967).

5. Jeremias, *Prayers of Jesus*, 111. This claim is disputed by D. Flusser, *Jesus* (New York, 1969).

6. Ibid., 111-12.

7. Guillet's book appeared in 1971 with the title *Jesus devant sa vie et son mort*; the ET was published in 1972.

8. See p. 43.

9. *Abba Pere!* (Rome, 1961). A thoroughly revised edition appeared in 1971, at which time he was able to draw from the largely corroborative work of Jeremias.

10. Along with a number of other exegetes who place these last words of Jesus within the context of the entire psalm, Marchel (n.1, p. 137) follows Benoit and Lyonnet in interpreting this cry of Jesus as a witness to his trust in his Father and in no way a cry of despair.

11. See p. 136.

12. Ibid., 167.

13. "Il ne s'agit pas la d'une conscience acquise, mais d'une conscience dont il jouit depuis toujours comme Fils de Dieu," ibid., 167.

14. *Jesus and the Spirit* (Philadelphia, 1975), 15-40; *Christology*, 22-33.

15. *Christology*, 27.

16. Ibid., 28.

17. Ibid.

18. Ibid., 32.

19. *Jesus and the Spirit*, 38. For a critique of Dunn's position and his response, cf. Jewett, *Christology and Exegesis*, 30.

20. *Jesus: An Experiment in Christology* (New York, 1979), 266.

21. Ibid., 267.

22. Ibid., 268.

23. J. Sobrino, *Christology at the Crossroads* (Maryknoll, N.Y., 1978).

24. Ibid., 174-75.

25. Ibid., 70-74.

26. Raymond E. Brown, Joseph A. Fitzmyer, Roland E. Murphy, eds., *The New Jerome Biblical Commentary* (Englewood Cliffs, N.J., 1990), 1323.

27. B. Malina, *The New Testament World* (Atlanta, 1981), 102.

28. This may well suggest, as we will see later in some detail, that the "Abba experience" of Jesus is the source of profound social revision, above all in forcing a basic reconsideration of "authority" and "power."

29. The word "aspect" is placed in quotes in recognition of the danger of falling into naive modalism at this point. What I am trying to express is the reality of God and Logos not being totally identical, for the Logos incarnated, that is, Jesus, experiences himself in relationship to his Abba who is distinct from himself. At the same time, I wish to stress the need to avoid imposing our human notion of "distinct" on the transcendent.

30. For now, the character and role of the transfiguration scene remains too ambiguous to use it as witness for the historical experience of Jesus or of his disciples. My own inclination is toward the view expressed by Werner Kelber in *The Kingdom in Mark* (Philadelphia, 1974), 71-82, which sees the transfiguration happening as the climactic event of revelation in the series of events that lead toward the passion of Jesus. From the perspective of gospel witness to *divine* intervention (revelation), the transfiguration scene stands clearly between and connecting baptism and Gethsemane. However, there is still support for the view that the passage in the synoptics is to be seen as an editorial retrojection of later resurrection faith. Cf. R. Stein, "Is the Transfiguration (Mark 9:22-29) a Misplaced Resurrection Account," *Journal of Biblical Literature* 95 (1976): 79-96. On the transfiguration, see also R. Pesch, *Das Markusevangelium*, vol. 2 (Freiburg, 1984), 69-84; H. Kee, "The Transfiguration in Mark: Epiphany or Apocalyptic Vision," in *Understanding the Sacred Texts*, ed. J. Reumann (Valley Forge, Pa., 1972), 135-52.

31. Cf. A. Feuillet, "Le bapteme de Jesus," *Revue biblique* 71 (1964): 321-52: "le recit du bapteme de Jesus remonte sans nul doute aux couches les plus anciennes de la tradition evangelique . . ." (321). See also J. Marshall, "Son of God or Servant of Yahweh," *New Testament Studies* 15 (1968/1969): 332-36; L. Hartmann, "Taufe, Geist und Sohnschaft," in *Jesus in der Verkundigung der Kirche*, ed. A. Fuchs (Linz, 1976), 95-96; R. Pesch, "Anfang des Evangeliums Jesu Christi," in *Die Zeit Jesu*, ed. G. Bornkamm and K. Rahner (Freiburg, 1970), 108-44.

dove — name for "beloved" in Canticle

32. "The rending of the heavens is a common feature of apocalyptic thought . . . ," V. Taylor, *The Gospel according to St. Mark* (London, 1952), 160, n.10.

33. Attempts to introduce the notion of "only son" do so on the basis of the possible typological connection with Isaac (Gen. 22:2); cf. J. Rademacher, *La bonne nouvelle de Jesus selon Saint Marc*, vol. 2 (Brussels, 1974), 61. See also A. Gaboury, "Deux fils uniques: Isaac et Jesus," in *Studia Evangelica*, vol. 4, ed. F. Cross (Berlin, 1968), 198-204; Taylor, *Gospel according to St. Mark*, 161. The idea of only-begotten is greatly strengthened, of course, if the alternative version of Luke's account, "You are my son, this day have I begotten you," is accepted as the original Lukan text; cf. A. Feuillet, "Bapteme de Jesus," 333-35.

34. Cf. "Le bapteme de Jesus," *Catholic Biblical Quarterly* 21 (1959): 483. This would agree with the application to Jesus of the Suffering Servant texts, for that application already implies Jesus' personification of the people Israel. For a somewhat different approach to linking Jesus to Israel in the baptismal scene, see P. Bretscher, "Exodus 4:22-23 and the Voice from Heaven," *Journal of Biblical Literature* 87 (1968): 301-10.

35. In line with his repeated stress on the community dimension of the baptism/temptation scene, Feuillet, *Recherches de science religieuse* 46 (1958): 524, links the dove symbolism to the new covenant people, drawing from the use of "dove" for the beloved in the Canticle.

36. Leander Keck, "The Spirit and the Dove," *New Testament Studies* 17 (1970/1971): 41-67.

37. Ibid.

38. Luke's use of the "dove" may have been influenced by his typological connection of Jesus in his baptism to the description of creation in *creation* Genesis.

39. Cf. Hartmann, "Taufe, Geist und Sohnschaft," 89-109. Hartmann traces the originating history of the text in conjunction with early baptism. See also his "Into the Name of Jesus," *New Testament Studies* 29 (1974): 21-48.

40. So, for example, Hartmann, "Taufe, Geist und Sohnschaft"; one argument adduced for the priority of *eklektos* is Luke's account of the voice from heaven in the transfiguration scene: "This is my son, my chosen one (*eklelegmenos*)."

41. On synoptic use of references to Old Testament passages, particularly in Isaiah, to identify Jesus as "son" or "servant," cf. W. Zimmerli and J. Jeremias, *The Servant of God*, rev. ed. (London, 1965), 80-106.

42. Cf. Marchel, *Abba*, 100-123. On the use of Abba in this passage he says: "Appartenant a une des sources les plus anciennes de la tradition synoptique, le mot Abba, en Marc 14,36, se presente comme une parole qui remonte a Jesus lui-meme . . ." (122).

43. Cf. K. Kuhn, "Jesus in Gethsemane," *Evangelische Theologie* 12 (1952/1953): 260-85. P. Benoit accepted the theory in his *Passion et resurrection*

du Seigneur (Paris, 1966), 30-32. J. Holleran, *The Synoptic Gethsemane* (Rome, 1973), 22-32, agrees substantially with Kuhn's position.

44. D. Stanley, *Jesus in Gethsemane* (New York, 1980), 108-22.

45. Ibid., 110.

46. If one wishes to ask whether Jesus anticipated his resurrection, the response would seem to come not in terms of any specific anticipation of what lay beyond, but in terms of his trust that his Father, being a faithful lover, would not leave him to death.

47. The possibility of the passage ascribing "divinity" to Jesus is linked also with the depicting of Jesus in relation to divine wisdom. To some extent the argument about a wisdom characterizing of Jesus revolves around the passage's connection with Sirach 51. Cf. J. Gnilka, *Das Matthaus Evangelium*, vol. 1 (Freiburg, 1986), 431-42; also A. Feuillet, "Jesus et la sagesse divine d'apres les evangiles synoptiques," *Revue biblique* 62 (1955): 166-96.

48. On the authenticity of the passage, cf. Jeremias, *Prayers of Jesus*, 45-48; A. Hunter, "Crux Criticorum — XI. 25-30, A Re-appraisal," *New Testament Studies* 8 (1961/1962): 241-43.

49. Accepting Q as the source of Matthew 11 and Luke 10:21, Grundmann in his commentary on Matthew, *Das Evangelium nach Matthaus* (Berlin, 1968), 815-19, distinguishes Matthew's more christological use of the passage from Luke's stress on the revelation of the Father. See also Marchel, *Abba*, 167, who emphasizes the scene as one of unique revelation, but as a revelation both of the Father and of Jesus as Son.

50. Cf. W. Grundmann, "Matth. XI.27 und die johanneischen 'der Vater-der Sohn'-Stellen," *New Testament Studies* 12 (1965/1966): 43.

51. For a general introduction to Jesus' parables, cf. R. Stein, *An Introduction to the Parables of Jesus* (Philadelphia, 1981); also J. Donahue, *The Gospel in Parable* (Philadelphia, 1988); B. Scott, *Hear Then the Parable* (Minneapolis, 1989).

52. Already in the early 1930s, Leonce de Grandmaison had highlighted the fact that Jesus' teaching, especially in the parables, is not teaching about himself (except indirectly) but about his "heavenly Father"; cf. *Jesus Christ*, vol. 2 (London, 1932), 34-86.

53. P. Ricoeur, "Biblical Hermeneutic," *Semeia* 4 (1975): 129-48, and esp. 30-33.

54. Out of the intense exegetical study of the parables that has marked the past few decades, the conclusion of Norman Perrin about the meaning of the key term "the kingdom of God" remains perhaps the most accepted: it is a tensive symbol that catches up into itself the myth/history of God's dealings with the chosen people and God's still unfulfilled effort to bring human history to its eschatological fulfillment. See Perrin's *Jesus and the Language of the Kingdom* (Philadelphia, 1976), 194-96.

55. J. Crossan, *In Parables* (New York, 1973), 15ff.

56. Much the same emphasis on the linkage of parables with experience is made by H. Weder, *Die Gleichnisse Jesu als Metaphern* (Göttingen, 1978),

94-96. "Die Nahe der Gottesherrschaft ist demnach als ein *Ereignis* zu denken, und zwar als *ein an die Person Jesu gebundenes* Ereignis . . . die Gleichnisse sind über ihr Subject, nämlich die Gottesherrschaft, mit der Person des historischen Jesus unlosbar verbunden" (95).

57. Cf. W. Grundmann, *Das Evangelium nach Matthaus* (Berlin, 1969), 459-64, and *Das Evangelium nach Markus* (Berlin, 1967), 318-25; X. Leon-Dufour, "La parabole des vignerons homicides," *Sciences ecclesiastiques* 17 (1965): 365-96; J. Jeremias, *The Parables of Jesus*, rev. ed. (London, 1963); W. Kümmel, "Das Gleichnis von den bösen Weingartnern," in *Aux sources de la tradition chretien*, ed. J. von Allmen (Neuchatel, 1950), 120-31; M. Hubaut, *La parabole des vignerons homicides* (Paris, 1976); K. Snodgrass, *The Parable of the Wicked Tenants* (Tübingen, 1983).

58. Cf. Snodgrass, *Wicked Tenants*, 3-40, who argues for the authenticity of the parable.

59. Ibid., 57-61.

60. For commentary on the parable, cf. Donahue, *Gospel in Parable*. Donahue points out that the view of God in this parable is antipatriarchal. See also J. Lambrecht, *tandis qu'Ill nous parlait* (Paris, 1980), 80-82, which provides a bibliography on Luke 15; E. Linnemann, *Jesus of the Parables* (New York, 1966), 73-80; R. Stein, *Introduction to the Parables*, 115-24; B. Scott, *Jesus, Symbol-Maker for the Kingdom* (Philadelphia, 1981), 47-58; Entreverses Group, *Signs and Parables* (Pittsburgh, 1978), 140-83.

61. Linnemann, *Jesus of the Parables*, 73-75.

62. "Obviously much of what Jesus says about shepherding both in John and the Synoptics reflects Ezek xxxiv. . . ," R. Brown, *The Gospel according to John*, vol. 1 (New York, 1966), 397. The impact of the Book of Ezekiel on early Christianity, especially upon the Johannine community, remains an intriguing but largely unexplored topic. At least to some extent this interest in Ezekiel 34 can be traced back to Jesus' own teaching.

63. On parables of the Good Shepherd, both in the synoptics and in John, cf. J. Quasten, "The Parable of the Good Shepherd," *Catholic Biblical Quarterly* 10 (1948): 1-12, 151-69; R. Brown, *Gospel according to John*, 1:383-400; B. Lindars, *The Gospel of John* (London, 1972), 352-64; A. Simonis, *Die Hirtenrede im Johannes-Evangelium* (Rome, 1967); C. Barrett, *The Gospel according to St. John* (New York, 1955), 304-14; E. Haenchen, *A Commentary on the Gospel of John*, vol. 2 (Philadelphia, 1984), 43-52; J. Dupont, "La parabole de la brebis perdue (Matt 18, 12-14; Lk 15, 4-7)," *Gregorianum* 47 (1968): 265-87, and "La parabole de la brebis perdue," *Ephemerides Theologicae Lovanienses* 40 (1975): 331-50; P.-R. Tragan, *La parabole du 'pasteur' et ses explications: Jean 10, 1-18* (Rome, 1980).

64. As mentioned earlier, Schillebeeckx develops this point at length in his *Jesus*, 256-71, as does Sobrino more implicitly in *Christology*, 67-74.

65. Most recently, exegetical opinion has moved away from the notion that the expectation of an imminent apocalyptic "end of the world" came from Jesus himself. Jesus probably had more of the eschatological view that typified Israel's great prophets, a view which recognized that the full

realization of God's kingdom still awaited future achievement but that granted history an unfolding role in that achievement. See J. Crossan, *In Parables*, 53-78; also N. Perrin, "Jesus and the Theology of the New Testament," *Journal of Religion* 64 (1984): 413-30.

Notes to Chapter 2

1. On the human limitations of Jesus' religious experience, cf. T. Corbishley, *The Prayer of Jesus* (New York, 1977). On reasons for a careful study of Jesus' background, see A. Wilder, p. 51, in W. Klassen and G. Snyder, *Current Issues in New Testament Interpretation* (New York, 1962). For an overall view of the religious outlook of first-century Palestinian Jews, cf. D. Flusser, "The Jewish Religion in the Second Temple Period," in *World History of the Jewish People*, vol. 8, ed. B. Netanyahu et al. (Brunswick, N.J., 1964), 3-40. While this present book was already in the process of editing, *The Religious World of Jesus* by my Holy Cross colleague, Frederick Murphy, was issued by Abingdon Press. Had Murphy's book been available earlier, it would have been one of the principle scholarly references for this chapter.

2. For an appreciative but somewhat critical review of Hengel's book, cf. F. Millar, "The Background to the Maccabean Revolution: Reflections on Martin Hengel's 'Judaism and Hellenism,'" *Journal of Jewish Studies* 29 (1978): 1-21. Prior to Hengel's work, attention had been drawn to the Hellenistic influences on Palestinian Judaism by Victor Tcherikover's *Hellenistic Civilization and the Jews* (Philadelphia, 1959).

3. The most extensive study of Galilee around the time of Jesus is that of S. Freyne, *Galilee from Alexander the Great to Hadrian* (Notre Dame, 1980). For an extended review of Freyne's book, cf. Eric Meyers, "Galilean Regionalism: A Reappraisal," in *Approaches to Ancient Judaism*, vol. 5, ed. W. Green (Atlanta, 1985), 115-31. Though it deals with a slightly later period, Martin Goodman's *State and Society in Roman Galilee, A.D. 132-212* (Totowa, N.J., 1983) is helpful in recreating the social situation of Jesus' day.

4. Cf. Freyne, *Galilee*, 194-200.

5. For a summary description of Sepphoris, cf. E. Schürer, *The History of the Jewish People in the Age of Jesus Christ*, vol. 2, rev. ed. by G. Vermes, F. Millar, M. Black (Edinburgh, 1979), 172-76. See also W. Bosen, *Galilaa als Lebensraum und Wirkungsfeld Jesu* (Freiburg, 1985), 69-75, for indications of Jesus' acquaintance with Sepphoris.

6. This may explain why a large number of priests fled from Judea to this area at the time of the first Roman war.

7. Freyne maintains that Galilee had remained predominantly Jewish and that there was no mass "conversion" under Antigonus.

8. On the fact that Galilee was observantly Jewish, though more flexibly so than Judea, cf. A. Oppenheimer, *The 'am ha-aretz* (Leiden, 1977).

9. On Yohanan's stay in Galilee (20-40 C.E.), cf. J. Neusner, *A Life of Yohanan ben Zakkai* (Leiden, 1970), 47-53.

10. D. Oakman, *Jesus and the Economic Questions of His Day* (Lewiston, Maine, 1986).

11. B. Lee, *The Galilean Jewishness of Jesus* (New York, 1988), esp. 79-83.

12. One can apply to Jesus the judgment of Lang regarding the prophetic experience: "The prophetic calling . . . is a real psychic event which, however, is prestructured and predefined by familiarization with the tradition. Convention and actual experience pervade one another and are fused in the event of the calling." B. Lang, *Monotheism and the Prophetic Minority* (Sheffield, 1983), 102.

13. On the possibility of the influence of Pharisaism on Jesus, Sanders, *Jesus and Judaism* (Philadelphia, 1985), quotes Morton Smith's *Jesus the Magician* (New York, 1978), 153-57: "There is strong evidence that there were practically no Pharisees in Galilee during Jesus' lifetime."

14. Cf. B. Meyer, *The Aims of Jesus* (London, 1979), 170-73.

15. For an intriguing study of Jesus' outlook and teaching in the context of his world, particularly in relation to emerging rabbinic Judaism, cf. J. Bowker, *The Religious Imagination and the Sense of God* (Oxford, 1978), esp. 121-38.

16. Lee, *Galilean Jewishness of Jesus*; cf. also Sanders, *Jesus and Judaism*.

17. The attempts of Brandon and Cullmann to link Jesus with the Zealot movement have been quite generally rejected. Cf. Freyne, *Galilee*, 216-29. At the same time, the Zealot movement itself needs some reassessment. M. Hengel, *Die Zeloten* (Leiden, 1976), 145-50, contends that Judas the Galilean's approach (beginning in the first decade of the common era) was religious rather than nationalistic and that the focus of his message was the lordship of God alone. The presumption of strong revolutionary currents in the Galilee of Jesus' day is even more strongly called into question by R. Horsley and J. Hanson in *Bandits, Prophets, and Messiahs* (San Francisco, 1985). There were popular uprisings, but these were more or less spontaneous reactions to repressive actions of Pontius Pilate.

On the broader context of "messianic" hopes at the time of Jesus, cf. P. Grelot, *L'esperance juive a l'heure de Jesus* (Paris, 1918), esp. 117-68, and more recently *Judaisms and Their Messiahs at the Turn of the Christian Era*, ed. J. Neusner, W. Green, W. Frerichs (Cambridge, 1987).

18. "There is clear evidence that he (Jesus) did not consider the Mosaic dispensation to be final or absolutely binding," Sanders, *Jesus and Judaism*, 267.

19. Freyne, *Galilee*, 259-97, points out that this agricultural aspect of Temple liturgy was an important factor in Galilean attachment to the Temple.

20. On the Shema and its accompanying benedictions, cf. M. McNamara, *Intertestamental Literature*, Old Testament Message, vol. 23 (Wilmington, Del., 1983), 194-99. A more detailed study of the origin, formulation, and historical use of the Shema and accompanying benedictions

is given by J. Petuchowshi, "The Liturgy of the Synagogue: History, Structure, and Contents," in *Approaches to Ancient Judaism*, vol. 4, ed. W. Green (Chico, Calif., 1984), 1-64.

21. Cf. S. Safrai and M. Stern, *The Jewish People in the First Century*, Compendia Rerum Iudaicarum ad Novum Testamentum, vol. 2 (Philadelphia, 1976), 800-801. On this Jewish practice of prescribed times for daily prayer as the root of the Christian liturgy of "the hours," cf. J. Jungmann, *The Early Liturgy* (Notre Dame, 1959), 98-99.

22. On the link of Hosea, Jeremiah, and Deuteronomy, see the two essays in *A Prophet to the Nations*, ed. L. Perdue and B. Kovacs (Winona Lake, Ind., 1984), by H. Cazelles, "Jeremiah and Deuteronomy," 89-112, and J. Hyatt, "Jeremiah and Deuteronomy," 113-28. A related essay in the same volume (313-24) is W. Holladay's "The Background of Jeremiah's Self-Understanding: Moses, Samuel, and Psalm 22."

23. On the existence of these two holidays in Jesus' time, cf. Safrai and Stern, *Jewish People in the First Century*, vol. 2, 851, 929.

24. On expectations of restoration as the prevailing context of Jesus' ministry, see Meyer, *Aims of Jesus*, 198-222, and Sanders, *Jesus and Judaism*, 116-19.

25. On the synagogue at the time of Jesus, cf. S. Safrai, "The Synagogue and Its Worship," in *The World History of the Jewish People*, vol. 8, ed. M. Avi-Yonah and Z. Baras (Jerusalem, 1977). See also Schürer, *History of the Jewish People*, vol. 2, 423-530.

26. Cf. E. Ebner, *Elementary Education in Ancient Israel* (New York, 1956); see also Hengel, *Judaism and Hellenism*, 78-83. Hengel points out that the procedures of the synagogue required a literate populace.

27. On the duties of the *hazzan*, including that of fill-in teacher, see Safrai, "Synagogue and Its Worship," 91-92. The fact that the legislation for universal elementary education was slightly later than the time of Jesus lessens somewhat the probability of his receiving such education in the Nazareth synagogue; but Safrai argues that schooling for boys ages seven to thirteen was widespread. This view is supported by Schürer, *History of the Jewish People*, vol. 2, 418: "It seems already by the time of Jesus the community also provided for the instruction of the young by establishing schools."

28. On the content of the education in the elementary synagogue schools, cf. Ebner, *Elementary Education*.

29. Cf. Lee, *Galilean Jewishness of Jesus*, 96-127.

30. Cf. A. Finkel, *The Pharisees and the Teacher of Nazareth* (Leiden, 1964); and more recently, H. Falk, *Jesus the Pharisee* (New York, 1985).

31. A later chapter on Jesus' prophetic consciousness will probe more deeply the differences between Jesus' mode of teaching and that of the Pharisaic rabbis.

32. On the various Gospel accounts of Jesus' relations to Pharisees, scribes, and Sadducees, cf. A. Saldarini, *Pharisees, Scribes, and Sadducees*

(Wilmington, Del., 1988), 144-98; also A. Finkel, *The Pharisees and the Teacher of Nazareth* (Leiden, 1964), esp. 129-36.

33. On the use of biblical texts in the synagogue service, cf. J. Mann, *The Bible as Read and Preached in the Old Synagogue* (New York, 1971); C. Perrot, *La lecture de la Bible* (Hildesheim, 1973).

34. On the synagogue service, cf. Safrai, "Synagogue and Its Worship," 65-98; also B. Reicke, *The New Testament Era* (Philadelphia, 1968), 120-24; and F. Manns, *La priere d'Israel a l'heure de Jesus* (Jerusalem, 1986).

35. Safrai, "Synagogue and Its Worship," 73.

36. See McNamara, *Intertestamental Literature*, 199-203.

37. Sanders, *Jesus and Judaism*, 61-76; somewhat earlier, B. Meyer, *Aims of Jesus*, 168-70, had pointed to the Temple cleansing's historically verifiable role in the events immediately leading to Jesus' death.

38. For a detailed description of Temple worship at the time of Jesus, cf. Safrai, "Synagogue and Its Worship," 282-337.

39. Clearly, many of the Psalms are themselves didactic, representing a major element in Israel's wisdom literature; and many others are a combination of proclamation and popular response.

40. Cf. Schürer, *History of the Jewish People*, vol. 2, 303.

41. Ibid., 304.

42. Ibid., 307.

43. Tabernacles was the commemoration of Israel's restoration after the catastrophe of the Babylonian conquest and exile. For a brief description of the ceremonies of Tabernacles, see Safrai and Stern, *Jewish People in the First Century*, vol. 2, 894-96.

44. Cf. Sanders, *Jesus and Judaism*, 116-19.

Notes to Chapter 3

1. This question has been dealt with in a number of essays during the past decade. See, e.g., E. Schüssler Fiorenza, "Towards a Feminist Biblical Hermeneutic," in *The Challenge of Liberation Theology*, ed. B. Mahan and L. Richesin (Maryknoll, N.Y., 1981), 107; R. Ruether, *Sexism and God-Talk* (Boston, 1983), 116-38; M. Cook, "The Image of Jesus as Liberating for Women," *Chicago Studies* 27 (1988): 136-50; A. Carr, *Transforming Grace* (San Francisco, 1988).

2. More than any other commentary on this masculine designation of divinity, Mary Daly's *Beyond God the Father* (Boston, 1973) drew attention to the patriarchal character of biblical language.

3. The classic text that injected the marriage imagery into the prophetic tradition and deeply influenced Deuteronomic theology was, of course, the early portion of Hosea.

4. Cf. P. Bird, "Women in the Old Testament," in *Religion and Sexism*, ed. R. Ruether (New York, 1974), 48-57.

5. For antipatriarchal elements in the Old Testament, cf. Ruether, *Sexism*, 61-68.

6. Cf. W. Albright, *From the Stone Age to Christianity* (Baltimore, 1940).

7. For a detailed study of the shift in the ancient Near East from dominance of goddess worship to patriarchal religion, cf. G. Lerner, *The Creation of Patriarchy* (New York, 1986), 141-98.

8. At the same time, one must remember that up to the time of the Babylonian exile much popular devotion continued to be directed to female divinities, even (according to Ezekiel's account) at times in the Temple itself.

9. It is interesting to speculate on the extent to which in the history of religions (and of thought movements antagonistic to religion) there is a basic division: religions that ultimately lead to pantheism and in which "God" and "nature" are coincident or religions that have a "transcendent" divinity who is the creator of nature. That leads to the further question, which bears on the present study: to what extent does the symbolism of the earth as female point away from a transcendent creator and in what way can present-day feminist theology find a deeper female symbolism coincident with transcendence?

10. Cf. 136-53 in vol. 1 of G.von Rad, *Old Testament Theology* (New York, 1962).

11. Cf. M. Hengel, *Judaism and Hellenism* (Philadelphia, 1974), 261-67. A more complex but not less important development is that in which ancient Mediterranean notions of "wisdom" were taken over and transformed in Judaism's development of the female figure of "divine wisdom"; Hengel (131-75) focuses his analysis of this in his study of Ben Sira's presentation of wisdom in relation to cosmic law.

12. On the lifelong study of the Torah by Jewish males, cf. S. Safrai, M. Stern, et al., *The Jewish People in the First Century*, vol. 2, Compendia Rerum Iudaicarum ad Novum Testamentum (Philadelphia, 1976), 945-70.

13. Ibid., 920-21.

14. This is a recurrent theme of the Psalms, e.g., Psalm 104. It is not clear how this imagery of "the wise man" resonated in people's imaginations at that time with the feminine personification of divine wisdom. Several present-day scholars are intrigued by the possibilities of recovering this image of feminine wisdom to balance out the patriarchal imaging of God that dominates the Bible. See E. Schüssler Fiorenza, *In Memory of Her* (New York, 1986), 130-40; E. Johnson, "The Incomprehensibility of God and the Image of God Male and Female," *Theological Studies* 45 (1984): 441-65; and Cook, "Image of Jesus." This is certainly helpful in the task of a constructive feminist theology, but the issue is not that clear when it is presented as the theology intrinsic to the biblical texts themselves. It is difficult to ascertain any antipatriarchal impact of the Old Testament figure of wisdom on Jesus himself, to say nothing of his contemporaries. While the identification of Jesus as divine wisdom is explicit in both Matthew and Luke and traceable to Q, the Gospel scene in question (Matthew 11) is that

of John's disciples coming to ask Jesus if he was the expected one; and what lies behind the Gospel narrative was probably Jesus' identification of himself as the "eschatological prophet" according to Isaiah 61. The key pre-Christian text influencing this tradition is Sirach, but as Hengel, *Judaism and Hellenism* (131-62), has argued in some detail, the Book of Sirach was influential in absorbing "preexistent wisdom" into the "preexistent law," thereby opposing female divinities and the Greek approach to *sophia*.

15. For a detailed study of the subordination of women in Israel's history and the canonization of that in the biblical texts, cf. A. Laffey, *An Introduction to the Old Testament: A Feminist Perspective* (Philadelphia, 1988). In *Memory of Her*, 105-18, Elisabeth Schüssler Fiorenza (following J. Plaskow) makes the salutary reservation that Christian scholars should not exaggerate the negativity of Jewish patriarchalism and notes that the actual situation of women may not have been as rigidly subordinate as the ideological formulation of legal prescriptions suggests. But she then goes on to detail the multifaceted marginalizing of Jewish women in the time of Jesus.

16. See Schüssler Fiorenza, *Memory of Her*, 119. Her conclusion (154): "The woman-identified man Jesus called forth a discipleship of equals that still needs to be discovered and realized by women and men today."

17. "A close examination of the Gospel traditions discloses already in the beginning of the tradition a tendency to play down the role of Mary Magdalene and the other women as witnesses and proclaimers of the Easter faith." E. Schüssler Fiorenza, "Feminist Theology as a Critical Theology of Liberation," *Theological Studies* 36 (1975): 625. See also in the same volume, 660-87, E. Carroll, "Women and Ministry," esp. 670-73.

18. See Cook, "Image of Jesus," 144-45.

19. On the presentation of Jesus' interaction with women in the Gospel of John, cf. R. Brown, "Roles of Women in the Fourth Gospel," *Theological Studies* 36 (1975): 688-99.

20. See Q. Quesnell, "The Women at Luke's Supper," in *Political Issues in Luke-Acts*, ed. R. Cassidy and P. Scharper (Maryknoll, N.Y., 1983), 59-79.

21. Cf. Schüssler Fiorenza, *Memory of Her*. At several points in the volume, Schüssler Fiorenza indicates the way in which the author of Luke-Acts, particularly in Acts, reflects a marginalizing of women already occurring in early Christian tradition.

22. One can think, for example, of the way in which at the beginning of Deutero Isaiah's "Book of Consolation," Yahweh, triumphant in battle against his rebellious people, leads them back from exile like a shepherd caring for his sheep, carrying the weak ones of the flock in his arms. Or again, the constant prophetic theme of Yahweh's concern for "the widows and orphans" and condemnation of those who exploit them.

23. A. Lourde, *Sister Outsider* (Trumansburg, N.Y., 1984), esp. 114-23; Mark Kline Taylor, *Remembering Esperanza* (Maryknoll, N.Y., 1990), 111-49.

24. This will be studied in more detail in chapter 5.

25. Cf. J. Donahue, "Jesus as the Parable of God," in *Interpreting the Gospels*, ed. J. Mays (Philadelphia, 1981), 148-67.

26. An important aspect of contemporary theology's turning to experience as its starting point has been the appeal to women's experience— clearly neglected up to this point in history by Christian theological reflection. As early as 1968, this was being voiced in professional circles in the U.S. See, e.g., the address by Pauline Turner, "The Contribution of Women to Theology," at the annual convention of the Society for the Catholic College Teachers of Sacred Doctrine (later renamed the College Theology Society). The use of experience as a starting point is now a widely accepted approach. For a recent statement of the position, see Ellen Leonard, "Experience as Source for Theology," *Proceedings of the Catholic Theological Society of America* 43 (1988): 44-61. In "Image of Jesus," Michael Cook emphasizes the importance of women's experience, but also suggests that within limits this can be shared vicariously by male theologians as a factor in their own reflection (137-41).

27. P. Kaminski, "Living Metaphors, Life-giving Symbols," *Theology and the University* 33 (1987): 69-85.

Notes to Chapter 4

1. Cf. J. Dunn, *Christology in the Making* (Philadelphia, 1980), 137; F. Snider, *Jesus der Prophet* (Göttingen, 1973), 257-60; and N. Perrin and L. Duling, *The New Testament*, 2d ed. (New York, 1982), 410-28.

2. On "prophet" as an ancient title for Jesus, cf. P. Benoit, "Les outrages a Jesus prophete," *Neotestamentica et Patristica* (Leiden, 1962), 107.

3. On Mark's redactional perspective in the scene of Peter's confession, cf. R. Pesch, *Das Markusevangelium*, vol. 2, 3d ed. (Freiburg, 1984), 27-36. Pesch provides (35-36) an extensive bibliography of studies on Mark 8:27-30.

4. On the historicity of Jesus' triumphal entry into Jerusalem on Palm Sunday and the probability that Jesus deliberately staged it as a claim to being king, see Sanders, *Jesus and Judaism* (Philadelphia, 1985), 306-8.

5. On Luke's theology of the Spirit's ongoing role in Christian history, cf. H. Flender, *St. Luke: Theologian of Redemptive History* (London, 1967).

6. Cf. Oscar Cullmann, *Christology of the New Testament* (New York, 1960), 27-47; also E. Cothenet, "Les Prophetes Chretiens dans l'Evangile selon saint Matthieu," in *L'Evangile selon Matthieu*, ed. M. Didier (Gembloux, 1972), 291; K. Berger, "Zum traditionsgeschichte Hintergrund Christologischer Hoheititle," in *New Testament Studies* 17 (1970): 393-400.

7. For a description of the literary forms prominent in Israel's prophets, cf. C. Westermann, *Basic Forms of Prophetic Speech* (Louisville, 1991); Westermann treats briefly Jesus' utilization of these forms. See also R. Meyer, *Der Prophet aus Galilaa* (Darmstadt, 1970), 12-18.

8. Cf. A Graffy, *A Prophet Confronts His People* (Rome, 1984), 123-29.

9. Westermann, *Basic Forms*, 128.

10. A lengthy treatment of Jesus' predictions is provided by F. Gils, *Jesus Prophete d'apres les Evangiles Synoptiques* (Louvain, 1957), 89-149.

11. On prophetic use of extraordinary imagery, cf. R. Wilson, "Prophecy in Crisis: The Call of Ezekiel," in *Interpreting the Prophets*, ed. J. Mays and P. Achtemeier (Philadelphia, 1987), 162-63. J. Donahue, *The Gospel in Parable* (Philadelphia, 1988), 15-20, expands on Dodd's description of Jesus' parables as "arresting the hearer by its vividness or strangeness, leaving the mind in sufficient doubt about its precise application to tease it into active thought."

12. Cf. J. Crossan, *In Parables* (San Francisco, 1985), on Jesus' outlook as that of prophetic eschatology rather than the apocalyptic outlook that was common in his day and basically influential in earliest Christian theology. Much the same conclusion is stated in Perrin and Duling, *New Testament*, 424-27.

13. On the origin of this usage in Jesus' own teaching, cf. Graffy, *Prophet Confronts*, 127.

14. A. Sand, *Das Gesetz und die Propheten* (Regensburg, 1974), points out that the use of the phrase "the law and the prophets" reflects the fact that what was in question was the law *as interpreted by the prophets*—which was the stance taken by the New Testament theologians and, prior to them, by Jesus himself.

15. Cf. Sanders, *Jesus and Judaism*, 61-90.

16. See Gils, *Jesus Prophete*, 49-77.

17. On the great prophets as interpreters of Israel's traditions, see R. Clements, *Prophecy and Covenant* (London, 1965), 25-26. Also Gils, *Jesus Prophete*, 156-59; he stresses Jesus' teaching as a prophetic interpretation of the previous Israelite prophetic traditions.

18. Cf. Gils, *Jesus Prophete*, 156-59.

19. Cf. L. Cerfaux, "Les paraboles de Jesus," *Nouvelle Revue Théologique* 55 (1928): 186-98.

20. On prophetic drawing from experience to portray God metaphorically, cf. B. Lang, *Monotheism and the Prophetic Minority* (Sheffield, 1983), 106-9.

21. J. Donahue has persuasively argued this exegesis of the parable in his *Gospel in Parable*, 52-57.

22. On the Israelite prophetic tradition of symbolic actions as "acted parables," cf. J. Sawyer, *Prophecy and the Prophets of the Old Testament* (Oxford, 1987), 10-11.

23. Cf. B. Meyer, *The Aims of Jesus* (London, 1979), 168.

24. On Jesus' awareness of prophetic vocation, cf. Snider, *Jesus der Prophet*, 257-60.

25. A valuable resource in sorting out the various questions regarding the historicity of Jesus' teaching and actions as they are depicted in the Gospels in the early portion of Ben Meyer's underappreciated book, *The Aims of Jesus*.

26. J. Gnilka, *Das Matthausevangelium*, vol. 1 (Freiburg, 1986), 80, argues that the basic difference in message—John's harsh picture of divine vengeance and Jesus' insistence on God's mercy—makes it very questionable that Jesus belonged to the circle of John's disciples. Others, e.g., Sanders, *Jesus and Judaism*, 91-92, incline toward the view that Jesus began his prophetic career as a disciple of the Baptist. An interesting perspective on Jesus' relationship to John is given by Guillet, *The Consciousness of Jesus*, (Baltimore, 1972), 45-46. After studying the way in which Jesus interpreted his own mission and career through reflecting on the prophetic texts with which he was familiar, Guillet suggests that this use of the Bible "took flesh" when Jesus actually encountered a prophet (John) in action.

27. See J. Dupont, *Etudes sur les evangiles synoptiques* (Louvain, 1985), 78-80. Also R. Tannehill, "The Mission of Jesus according to Luke IV 16-30," in E. Grasser, A. Strobel, R. Tannehill, and W. Eltester, *Jesus in Nazareth* (Berlin, 1972), 51-75.

28. For a lengthy defense of the historicity of Jesus' response to John's disciples, cf. W. Kümmel, "Jesu Antwort an Johannes den Taufer," in *Heilsgeschehen und Geschichte*, vol. 2 (Marburg, 1978), 177-200.

29. So J. Jeremias, *The Proclamation of Jesus*, vol. 1 in his *New Testament Theology* (New York, 1971); V. Taylor, *Jesus and His Sacrifice* (London, 1937), 47-48; T. W. Manson, *Jesus the Messiah* (London, 1948), 110-13.

30. See Sanders, *Jesus and Judaism*, 332-33; his opinion is strongly influenced (as he himself remarks) by the views of C. K. Barrett.

31. V. Taylor, *Jesus and His Sacrifice*, 46. On the link between Jesus' awareness of impending death and his self-identification as prophet, see Snider, *Jesus der Prophet*, 257-59.

32. Cf. H. J. Steichele, *Der leidende Sohn Gottes* (Regensburg, 1980), 192-279. Steichele develops at length the connections between Mark's passion narrative and Psalm 22. A. Higgins, *Jesus and the Son of Man* (London, 1964), rejects this limitation of Jesus' awareness to simply "the righteous one": "Jesus' fundamental understanding of his mission thus went far beyond (though it may have included it as a secondary element) the thought of the humiliation and exaltation of the righteous in contemporary Judaism. It was conditioned by a much more profound consideration—the consciousness of his sonship to the Father, Abba" (208).

33. "We may conclude that Jesus sensed an *eschatological uniqueness* in his relationship to God—as the one whose ministry was the climax to God's purposes for Israel . . . ," Dunn, *Christology*, 28.

34. See J. Kingsbury, *The Christology of Mark's Gospel* (Philadelphia, 1983), esp. 168-73. See also J. Fitzmyer, *The Gospel according to Luke, I-IX* (Garden City, N.Y., 1979), 208-11, for a somewhat different view which, however, does not seem to rule out Kingsbury's position. An interesting view that brings together the link of "Son of Man" with Daniel 7 and Jesus' use of the term to emphasize his humanity is provided by J. Bowker, *The Religious Imagination and the Sense of God* (Oxford, 1978), 156-69.

35. A different interpretation of Daniel 7 is provided by J. Collins, "Apocalyptic Eschatology as the Transcendence of Death," *Catholic Biblical Quarterly* 36 (1974): 21-43, who sees the figure of Son of Man as a heavenly patron of Israel, probably Michael. However, this does not seem to take account of the fact that later in the same chapter of Daniel, the exact promise given "the Son of Man" is now given to the Jewish people.

36. On the prophetic vocation experience, cf. W. Zimmerli, *Ezekiel*, vol. 1 (Philadelphia, 1979), 97-100.

37. Cf. J. Lindblom, *Prophecy in Ancient Israel* (Philadelphia, 1962), 105-48, 173-97; J. Sawyer, *Prophecy and the Prophets of the Old Testament* (Oxford, 1987), 3-5; R. Wilson, "Prophecy in Crisis," 160-67.

38. Cf. W. Brueggemann, "The Book of Jeremiah: Portrait of the Prophet," in *Interpreting the Prophets*, ed. J. Mays and P. Achtemeier (Philadelphia, 1987), 113-29.

39. Ibid., 120-27.

40. Ibid., 120-24.

41. Cf. Steichele, *Der leidende Sohn Gottes*, 41-70; also L. Keck, "The Introduction to Mark's Gospel," *New Testament Studies* 12 (1955/1956): 352-70.

42. Cf. Gnilka, *Matthausevangelium*, 80-81; E. Schweizer, *Beitrage zur Theologie des Neuen Testaments* (Zürich, 1970), 80.

43. Cf. B. Rigaux, *Temoignage de l'evangile de Luc* (Brussels, 1970), 365-73.

44. Cf. Schweizer, *Beitrage zur Theologie des Neuen Testaments*, 79; also Steichele, *Der leidende Sohn Gottes*, 192-279, who does not develop the Servant theme in discussing the baptism—he is more interested in the use of "Son of God" in this context—but in an analysis of Mark 15:2-41, he understands the use of Psalm 22 as descriptive of Jesus as "the suffering just one."

45. See G. Sloyan, *Jesus on Trial* (Philadelphia, 1973), a critical but irenic analysis of the available evidence and of recent studies of the process of Jesus' condemnation to death.

46. See Sanders, *Jesus and Judaism*, 270-318; also P. Benoit, "Les outrages a Jesus Prophete (Mc xiv 65 par)," in *Neotestamentica et Patristica*, Festschrift for O. Cullmann (Leiden, 1962), 92-110.

47. Cf. Sanders, *Jesus and Judaism*, 98-106.

48. Cf. B. Meyer, *Aims of Jesus*, 169.

49. 'The twelve' as such evoked restoration motifs that had stamped the hopes of Israel since the days of Ezekiel," ibid., 173. See also G. Schneider, "Die zwölf Apostel als Zeugen," in *Lukas, Theologe der Heilsgeschichte* (Bonn, 1985), 61-85.

Notes to Chapter 5

1. On the interpretation of Phil. 2:8 and the nature of Christ's obedience, cf. R. Martin, *Carmen Christi* (Cambridge, 1967), 197-228.

2. On "obedience" as used in this passage and understood by Paul in relation to other key ideas like justification and freedom, see E. Käsemann, *Commentary on Romans* (Grand Rapids, 1980), 155-86.

3. G. Hughes, *Hebrews and Hermeneutics* (Cambridge, 1979), 177, n.66.

4. On the background Jewish use, cf. *upakoe* in G. Kittel and G. Friedrich, eds., *Theological Dictionary of the New Testament*, vol. 1 (Grand Rapids, Mich., 1964), 224-25.

5. J. Jeremias, *New Testament Theology*, vol. 1 (New York, 1971), 276-99. F. Hahn, whose position on this question has been particularly influential, argues that the title "Servant" does not originate with Jesus himself; see *The Titles of Jesus in Christology* (New York, 1969), 54-63. However, Jesus' explicit application to himself of the title is not the same thing as seeing himself fulfilling the prophetic ideal sketched in the Servant Songs.

6. See W. Zimmerli and J. Jeremias, *The Servant of God*, rev. ed. (London, 1965), 25-35.

7. See esp. J. Dunn, *Jesus and the Spirit* (Philadelphia, 1979), 41-49.

8. On the questions raised for Jesus' contemporaries by the earlier Jewish-Israelitic use of "spirit," cf. E. Schweizer, *The Holy Spirit*, a slight revision in monograph form of the article *"pneuma,"* published earlier in the *Theological Dictionary of the New Testament* (Philadelphia, 1980), 29-45. For a detailed study of the Hebrew Bible's use of "spirit," cf. P. van Imschoot, *Theologie de l'Ancien Testament* (Paris, 1954), 183-200. A more recent brief but compressed and helpful treatment is that of Y. Congar, *I Believe in the Holy Spirit*, vol. 1 (New York, 1983), 3-14.

9. Congar, *I Believe*, vol. 1., 10.

10. See G. Johnston, *The Spirit-Paraclete in the Gospel of John* (Cambridge, 1970). J. Dunn, on the other hand, draws more from the synoptic accounts of Jesus as a charismatic healer and from the parallels with the early Christian charismatic experience as witnessed to by Acts and by the Pauline literature. Cf. *Jesus and the Spirit*, 68-92, 157-70.

11. On the link between Jesus' sense of possessing Spirit-power and his awareness of being the eschatological prophet, see Dunn, *Jesus and the Spirit*, 47-48.

12. On the synoptic use of these two terms, cf. C. K. Barrett, *The Holy Spirit and the Gospel Tradition* (London, 1966), 69-93.

13. 1 Kings 22:19-23.

14. J. Dunn's remarks on this point are worth citing: "I am suggesting that Jesus' self-consciousness was a lot less clear cut and structured than is frequently supposed. The concepts he used when speaking of himself were more fluid, more inchoate, than talk of 'titles' would suggest. So far as his relation to God was concerned, the concept of 'son' to God as Father was basic and most appropriate; just as in his relation to men his chosen self-reference seems to have been *bar nasa* . . . With Jesus, in short, we see the freshness of an original mind, a new spirit, taking up old categories and concepts, remoulding them, creating them afresh, using them in a wholly new way in the light of his basic experience of God caring and

126

commanding him and of being bound to God by the closest ties of love and obedience" (Dunn, *Jesus and the Spirit*, 40).

15. "When Jesus speaks about God in parables, he does so because God is for him a living God who speaks to us ever anew . . . ," E. Schweizer, *The Holy Spirit*, 85. On the parables, their character and interpretation, see J. Donahue, *The Gospel in Parable* (Philadelphia, 1988); also B. Scott, *Hear Then the Parable: A Commentary on the Parables of Jesus* (Philadelphia, 1989).

16. Cf. Donahue, *Gospel in Parable*, 146-58.

17. Though some aspects of her description of Jesus' historical experience would not stand up to more recent critical study of the New Testament, Adrienne von Speyr's *Penance* (New York, 1964) remains one of the more insightful reflections on Jesus' experience of evil.

18. On Jesus' "woe statements," cf. Jeremias, *New Testament Theology*, vol. 1, 141-51. Though recent scholarship indicates that attributing opposition to Jesus' teaching to "the scribes and Pharisees" may say more about the conflict encountered by early Christians, e.g., the community out of which the Gospel of Matthew emerged, than about the identity of those who opposed Jesus himself, there seems little doubt that Jesus encountered opposition and criticism from some of the Pharisaic teachers of his day, more probably from the school of Shammai. Cf. B. Lee, *The Galilean Jewishness of Jesus* (New York, 1988), 99-127.

19. On Jesus as a charismatic healer, cf. Dunn, *Jesus and the Spirit*, 69-76.

INDEX

fundamental question: Who do you say I am?
   Answer indicates entire understanding
                          • of Vanity
                          • of self
                          • of human life
                          - of history
                          • of God
Modern science (social & phy.) provided
new tools to deal w. question. (psychology
                                   Sociology
                                   history   etc.
                                   anthropology

Jesus is NORMATIVE
      for Christians
      as a WAY to God